The Booklover

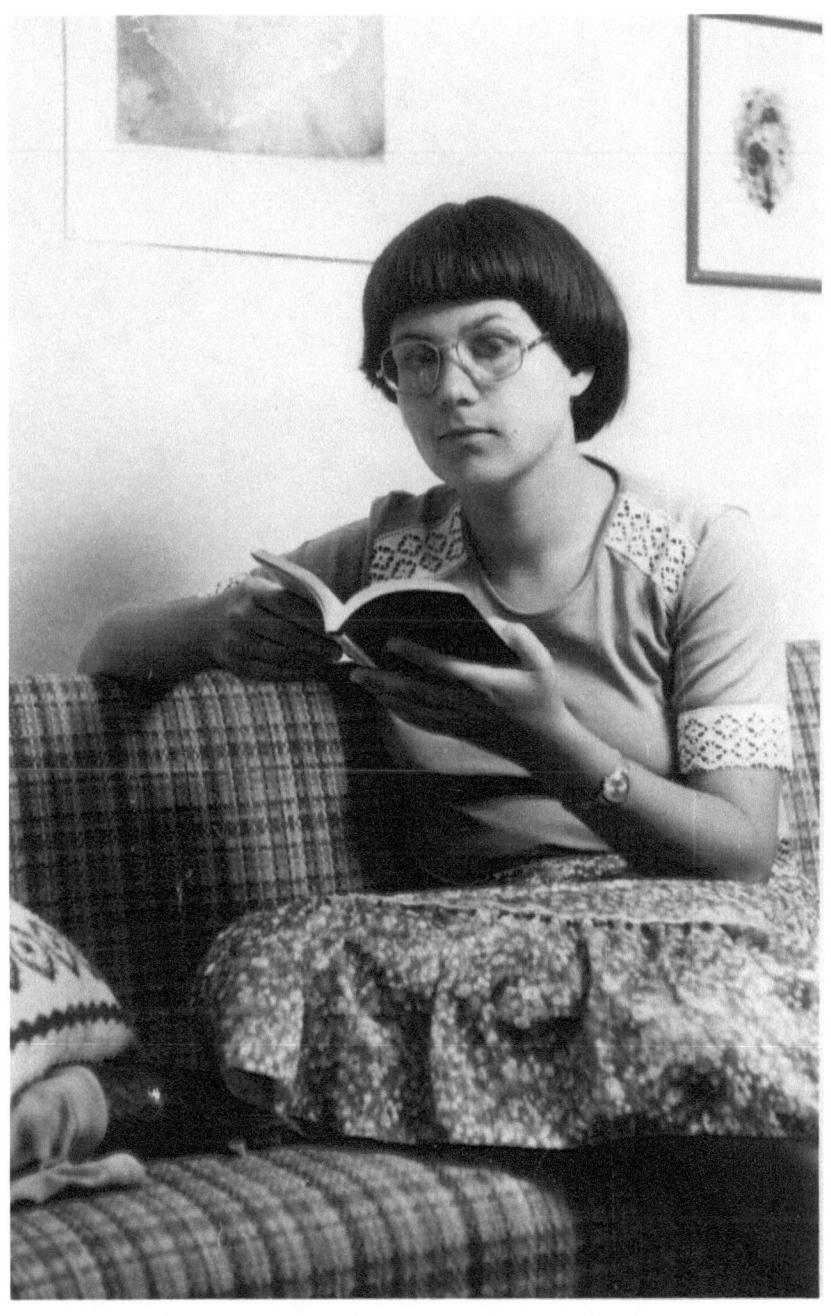

Kippenberger
Psychobuildings

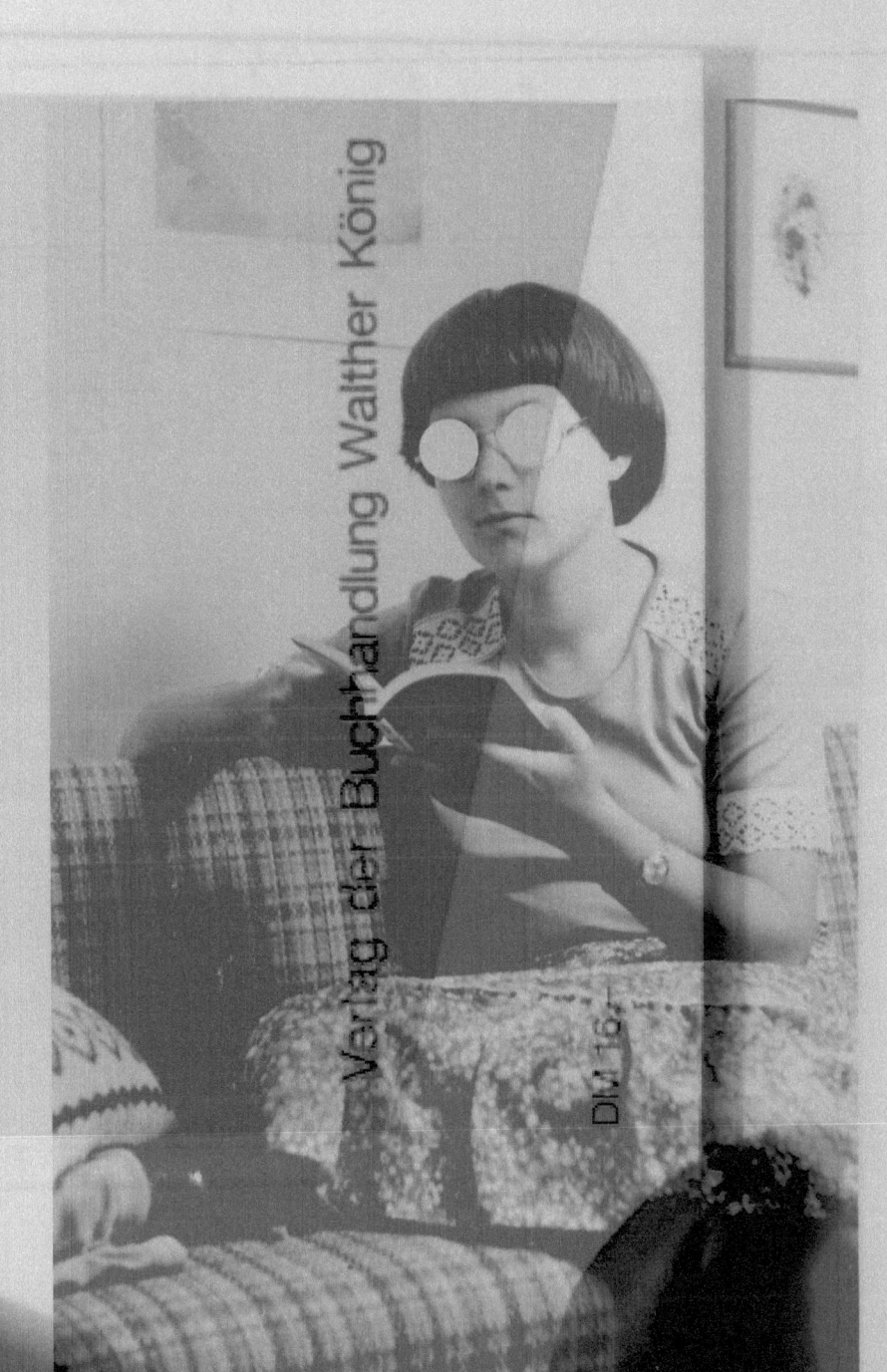

Verlag der Buchhandlung Walther König

DM 16,-

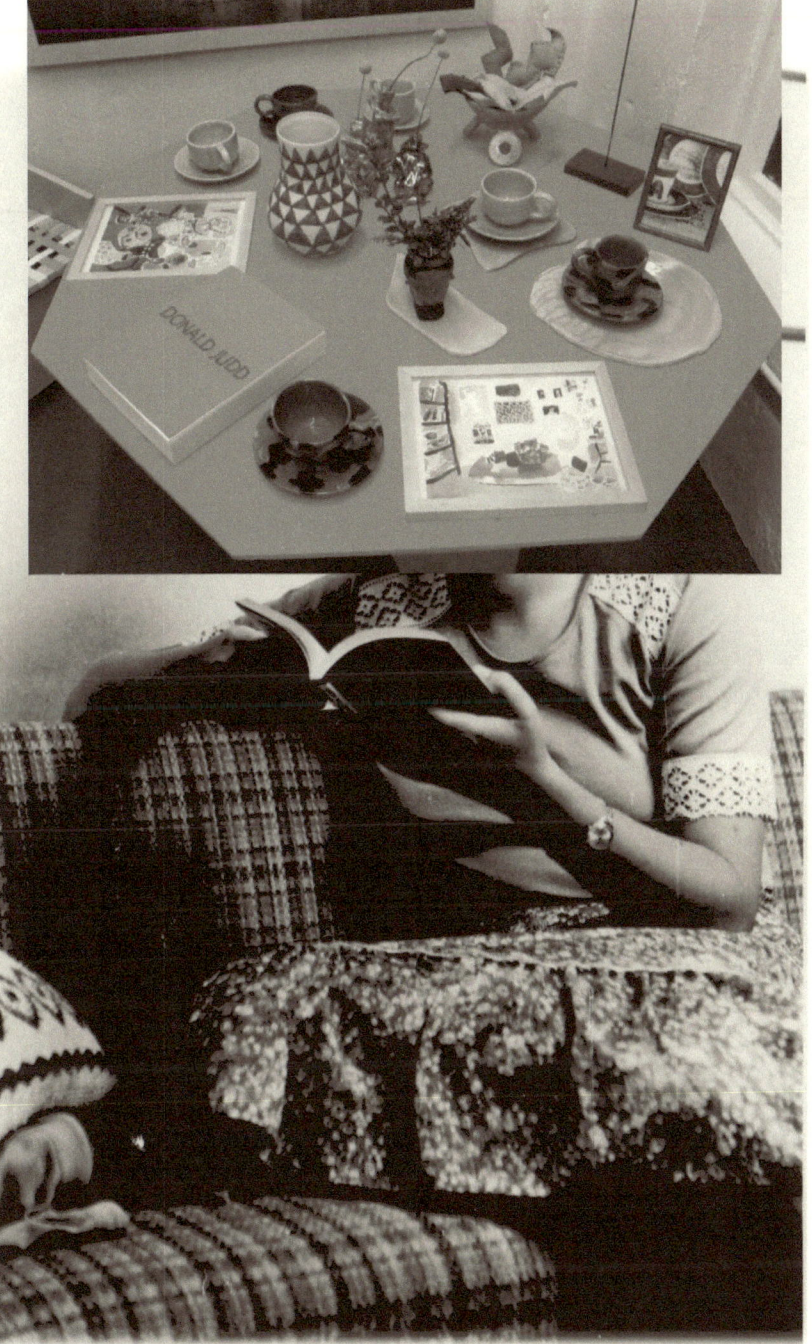

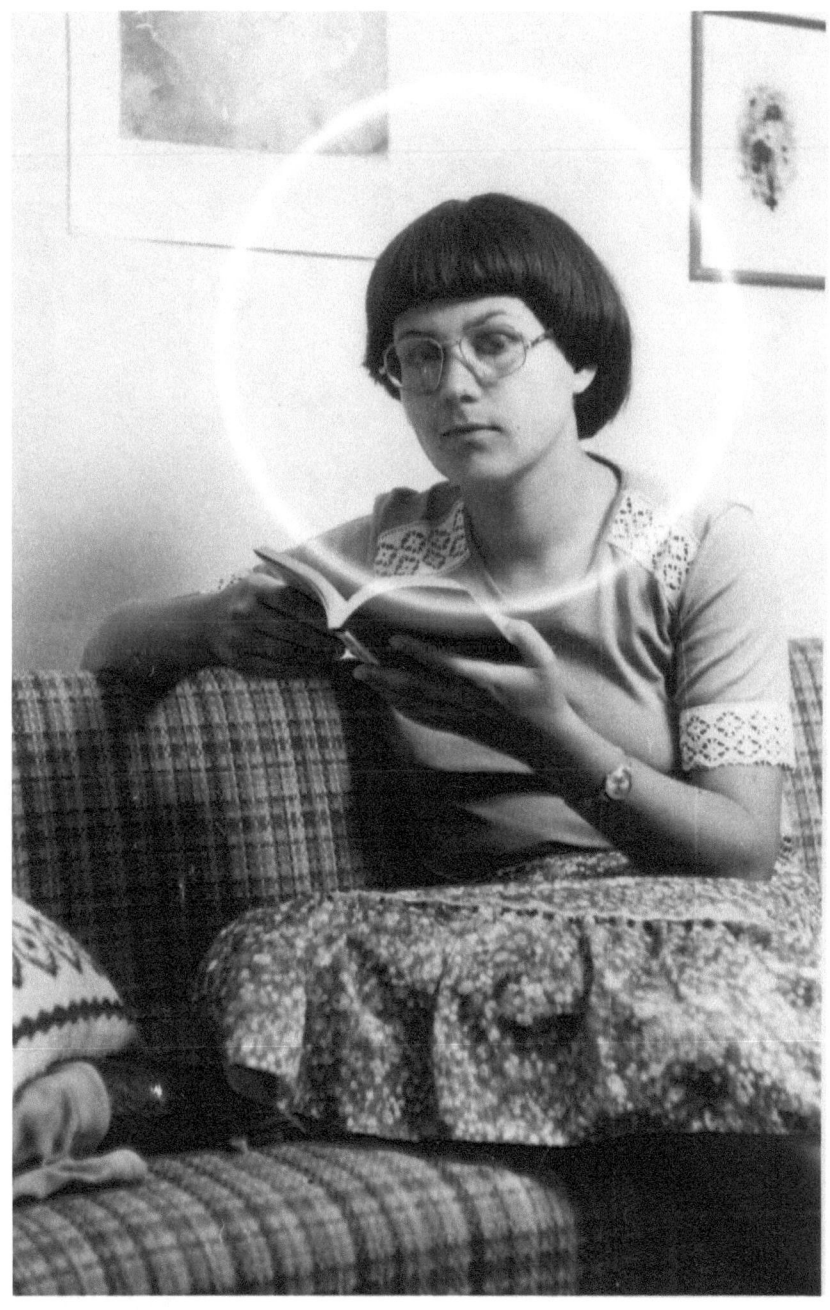

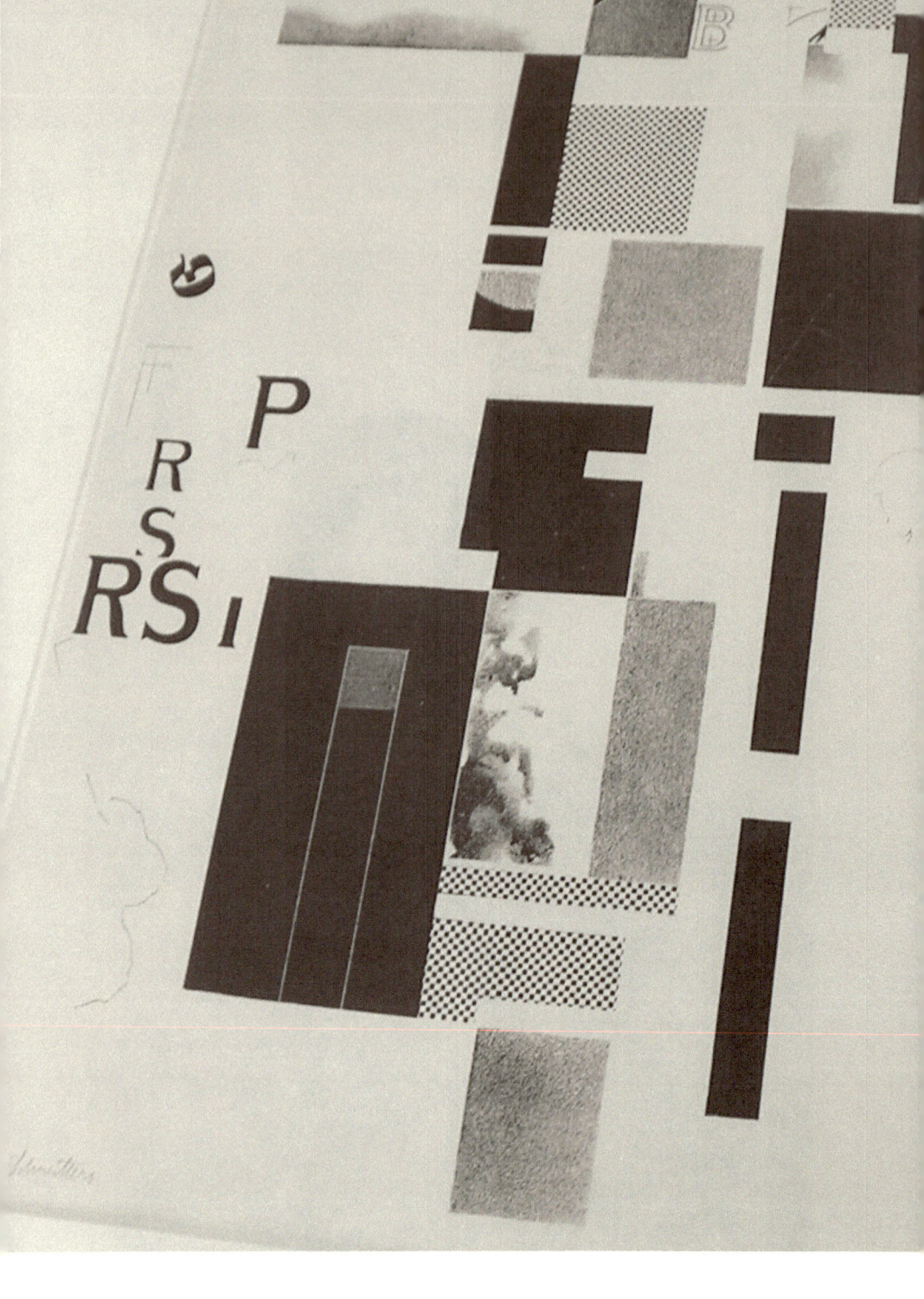

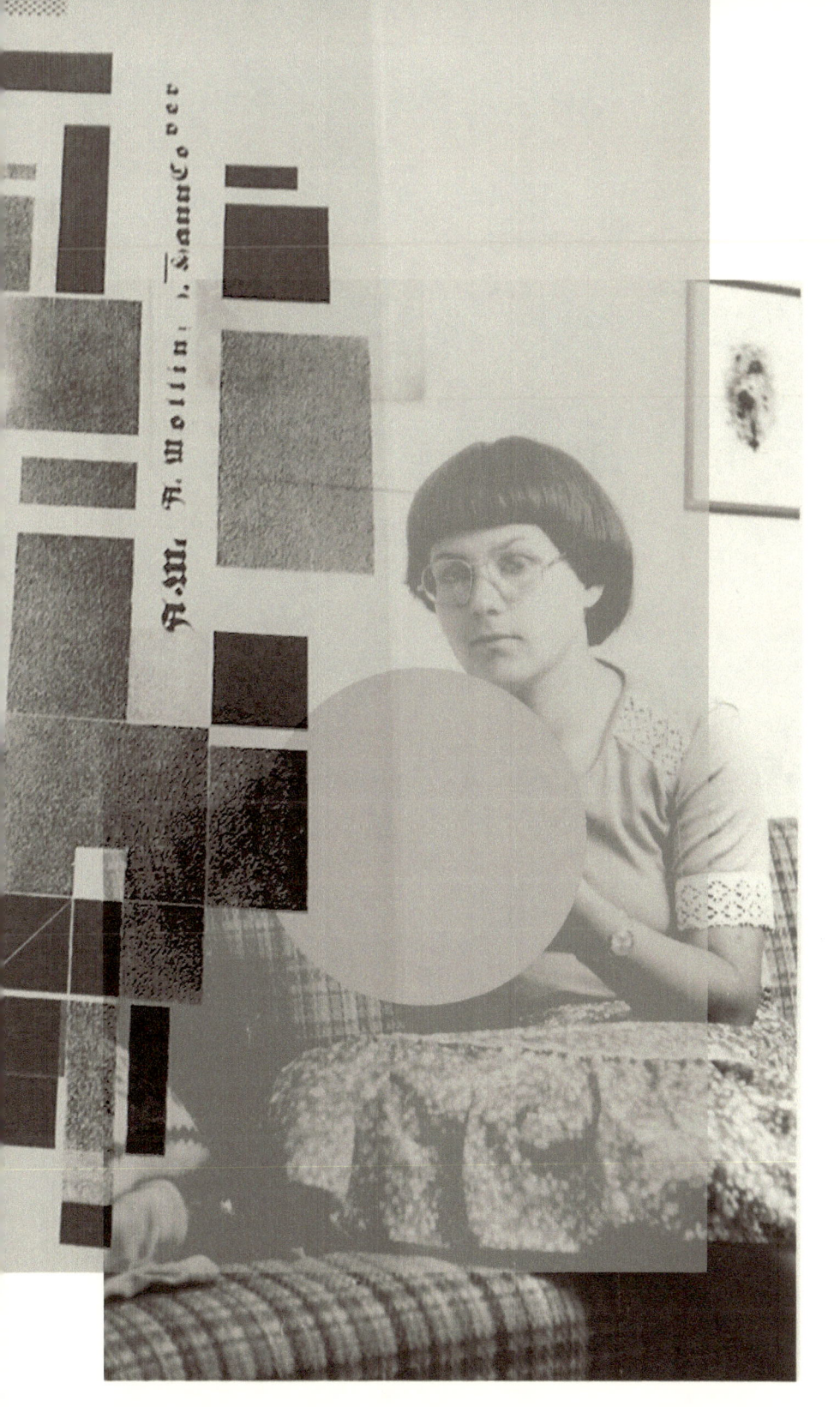

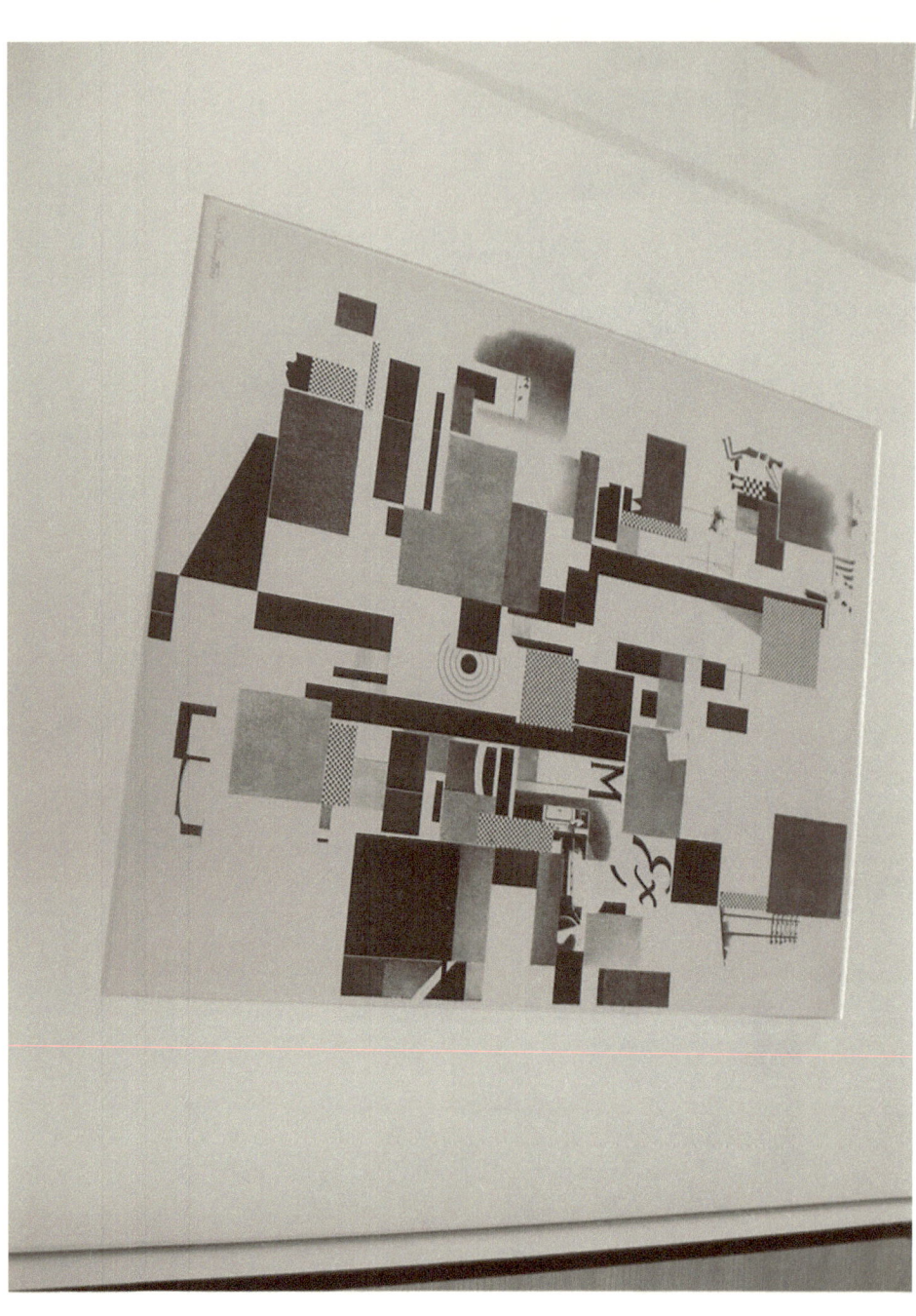

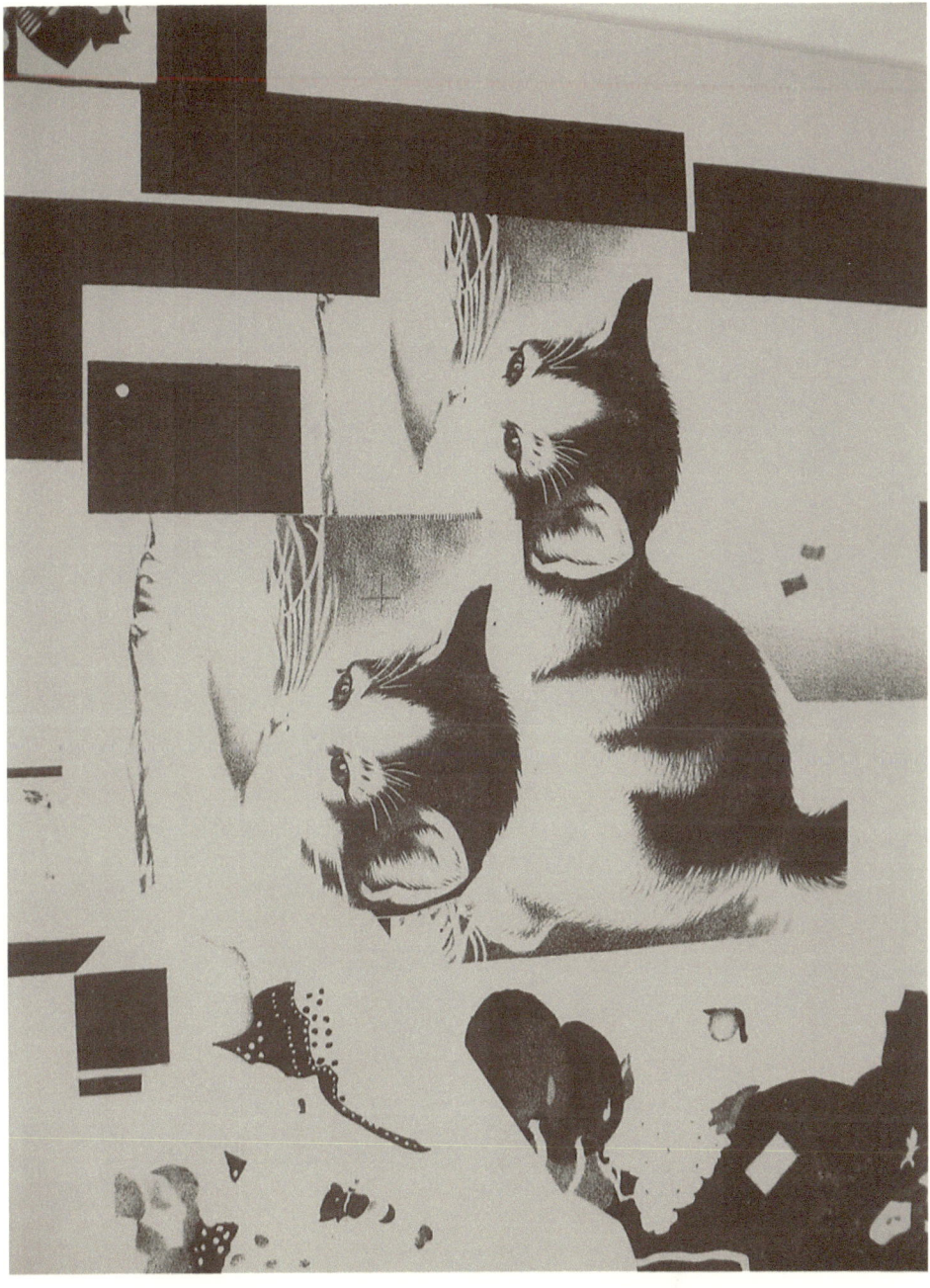

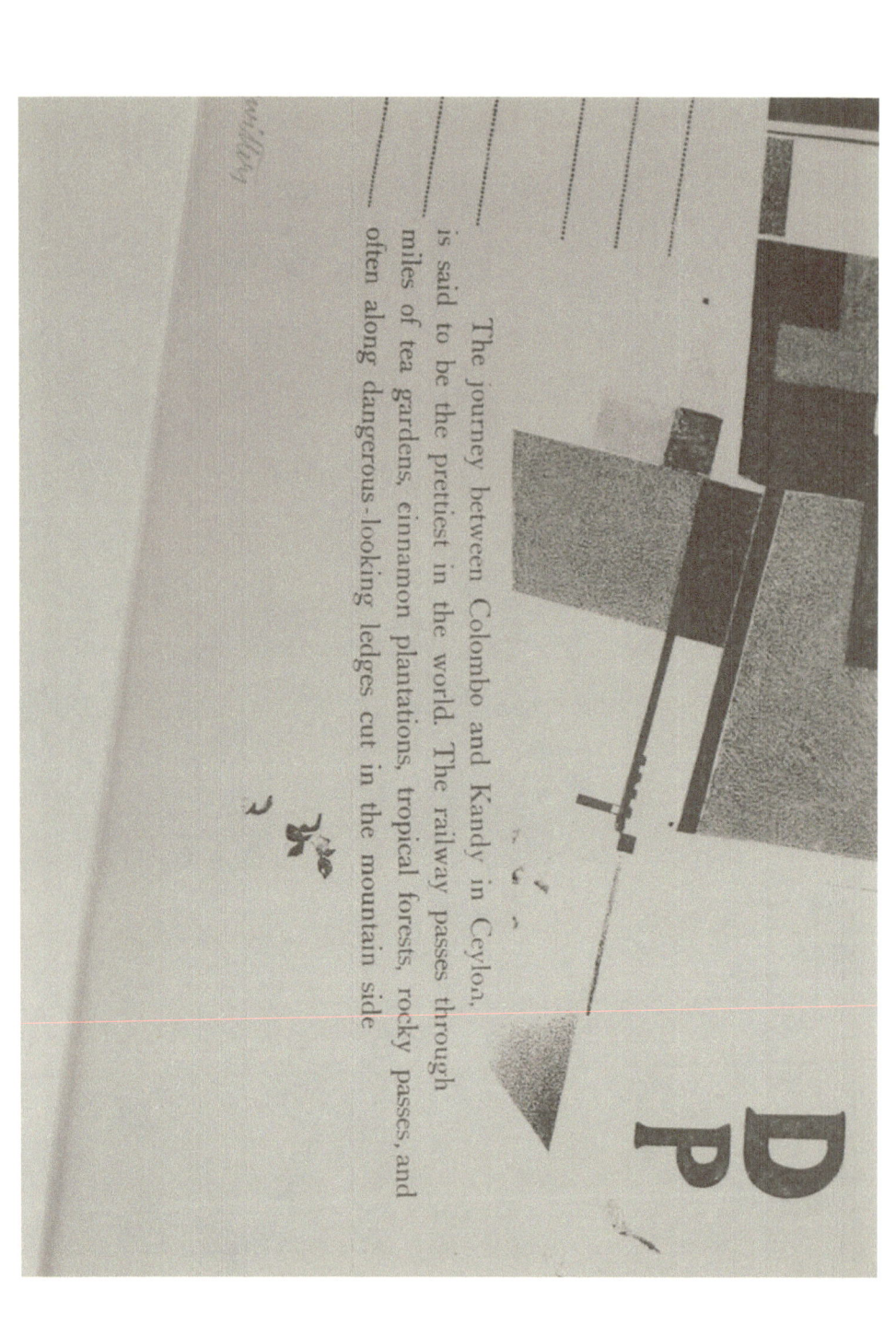

The journey between Colombo and Kandy in Ceylon, is said to be the prettiest in the world. The railway passes through miles of tea gardens, cinnamon plantations, tropical forests, rocky passes, and often along dangerous-looking ledges cut in the mountain side

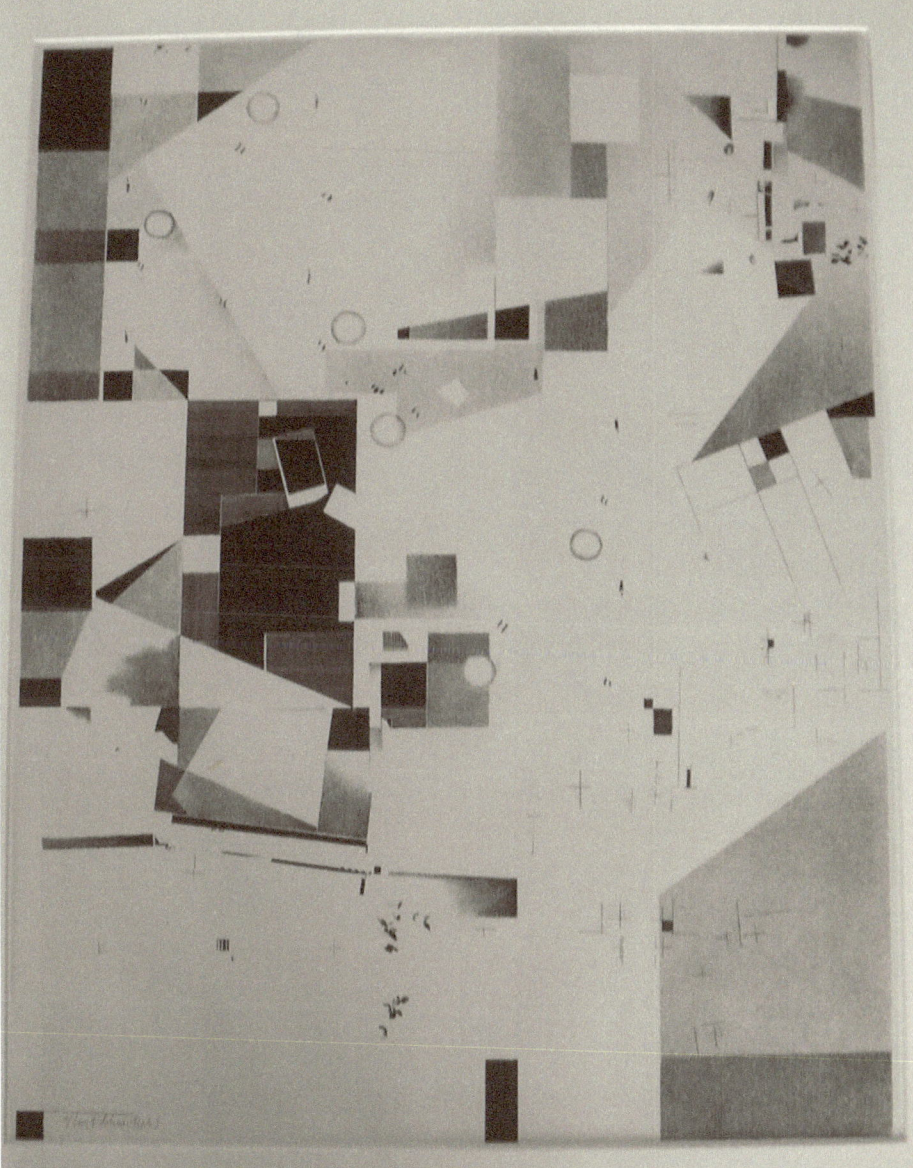

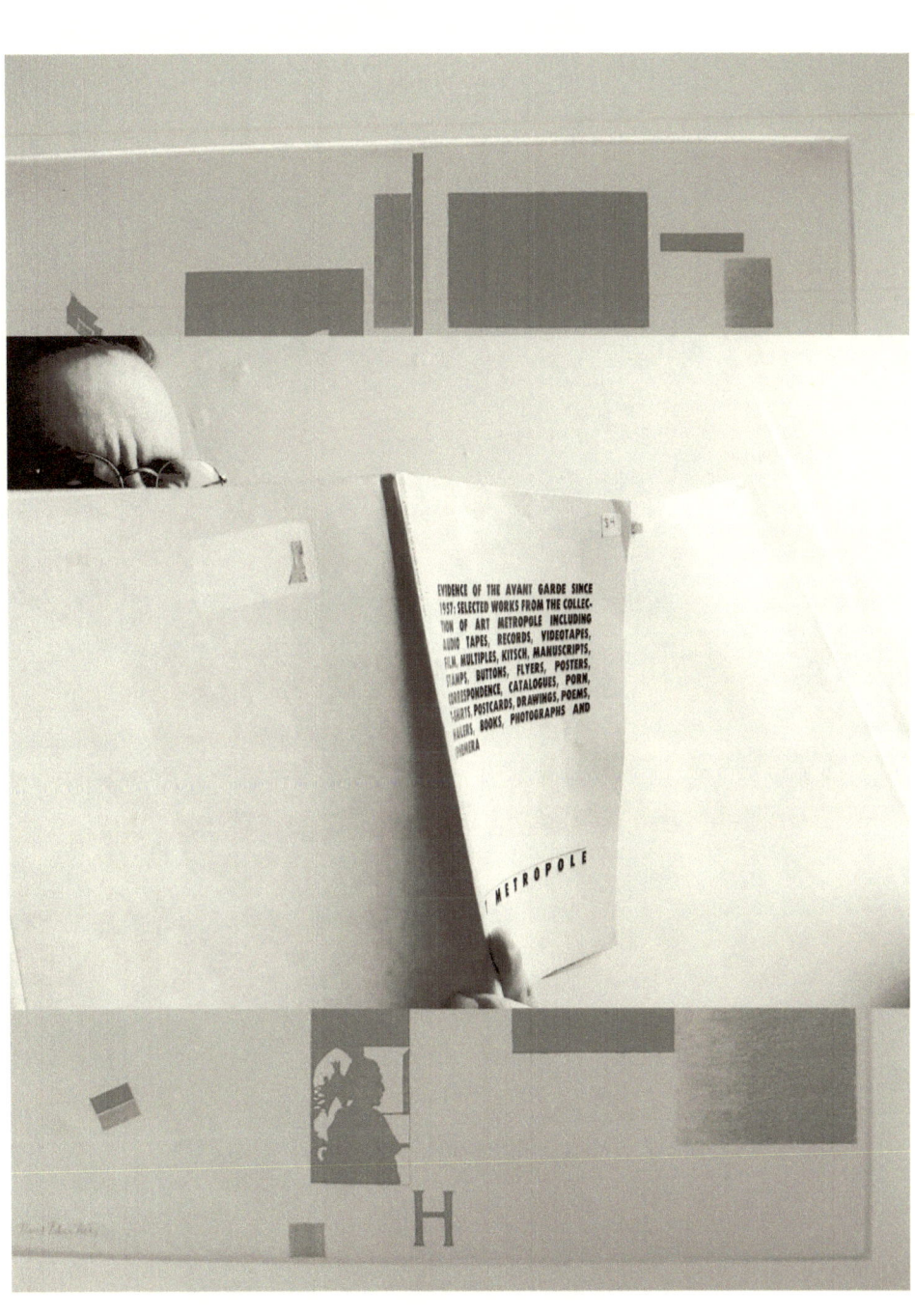

EVIDENCE OF THE AVANT GARDE SINCE
1957: SELECTED WORKS FROM THE COLLEC-
TION OF ART METROPOLE INCLUDING
AUDIO TAPES, RECORDS, VIDEOTAPES,
FILM, MULTIPLES, KITSCH, MANUSCRIPTS,
STAMPS, BUTTONS, FLYERS, POSTERS,
CORRESPONDENCE, CATALOGUES, PORN,
T-SHIRTS, POSTCARDS, DRAWINGS, POEMS,
XEROXES, BOOKS, PHOTOGRAPHS AND
EPHEMERA

METROPOLE

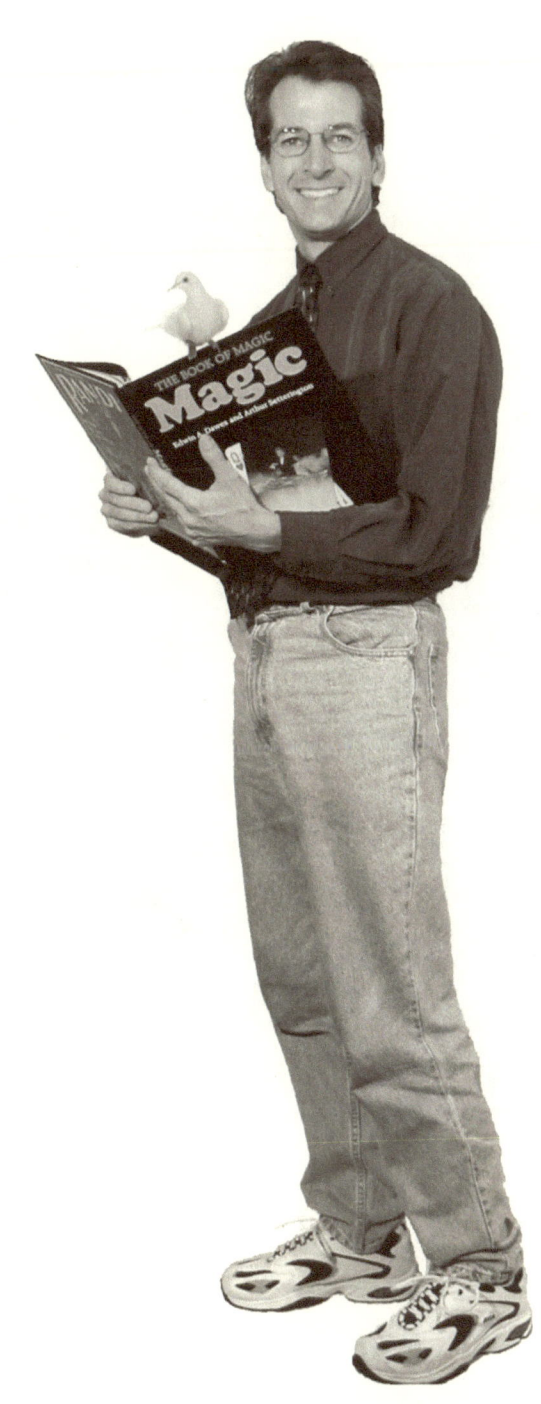

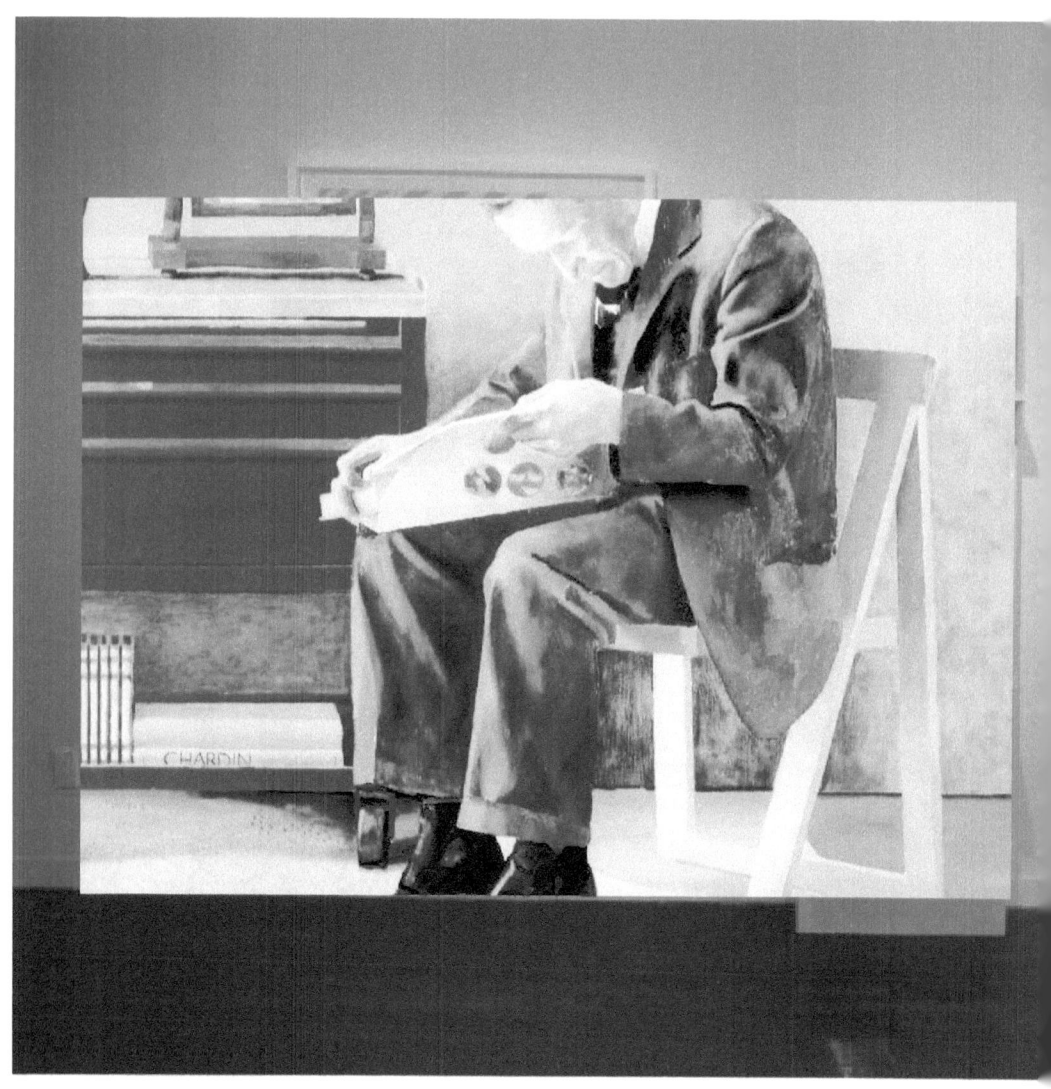

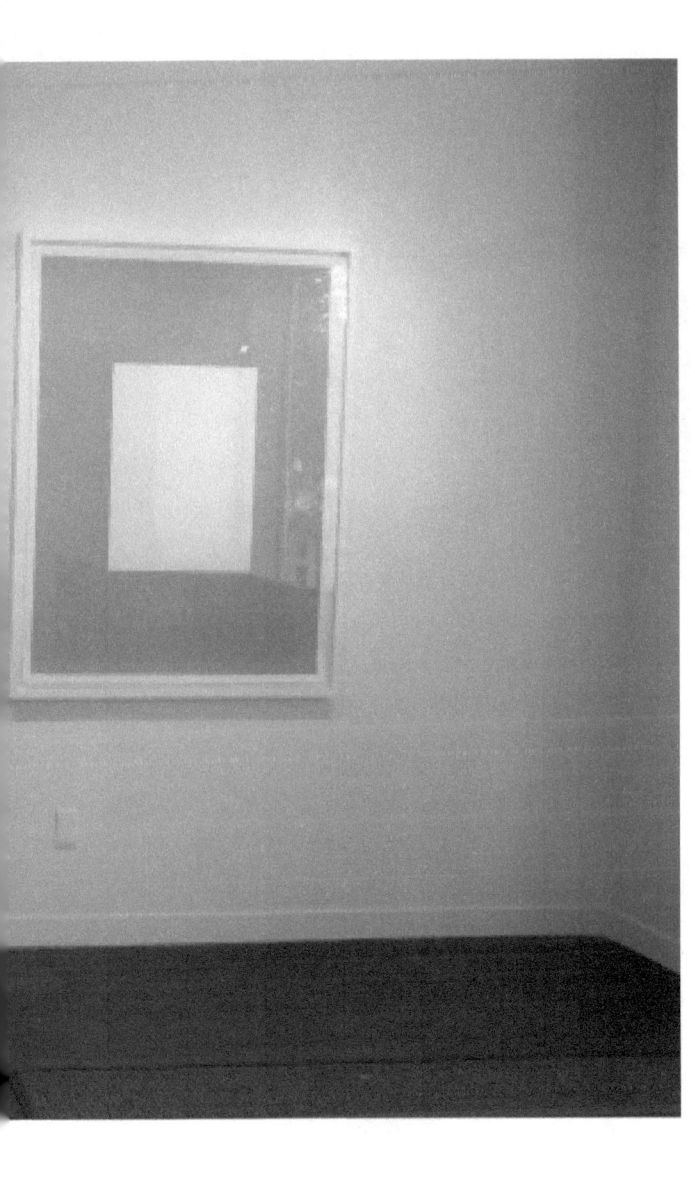

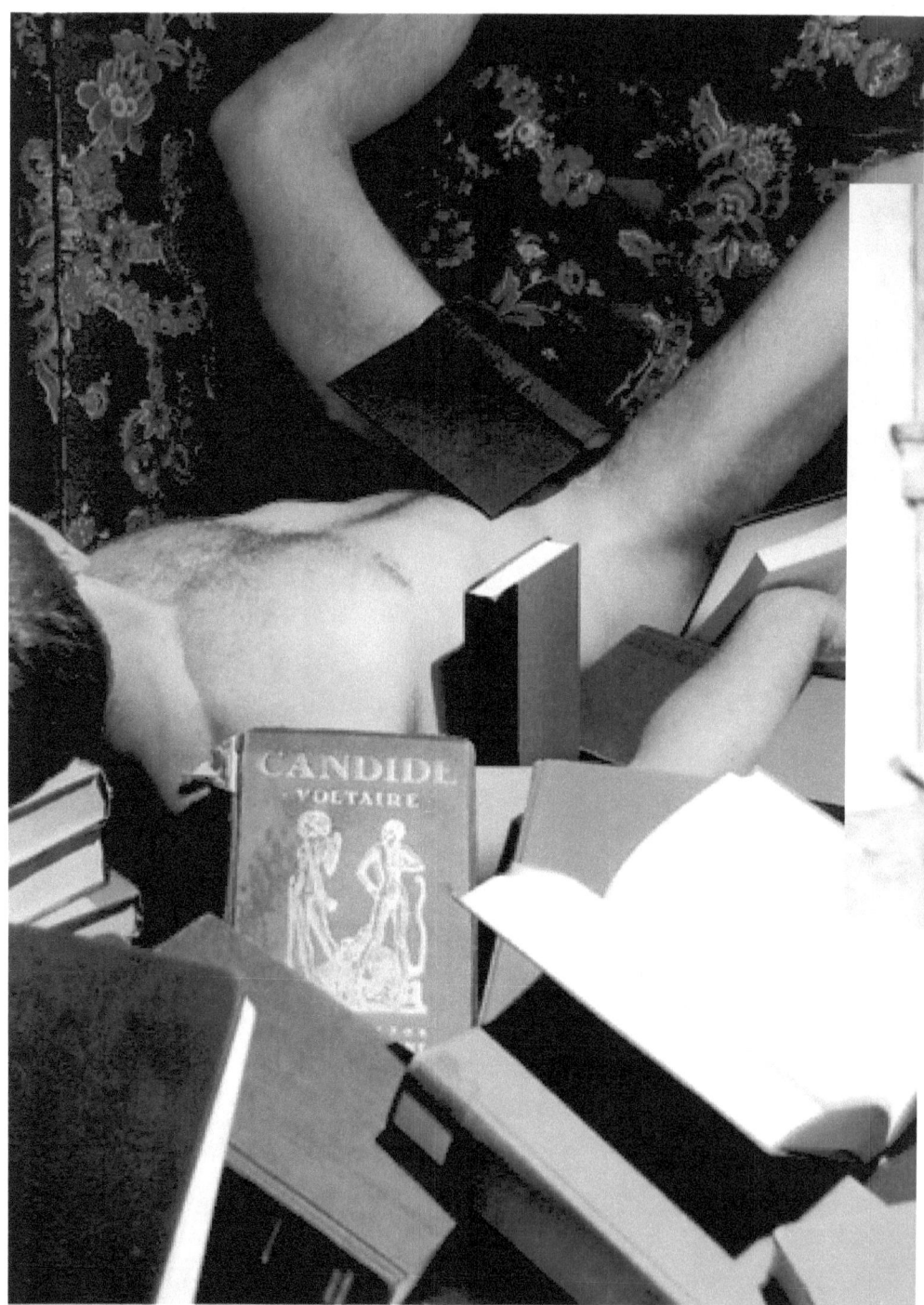

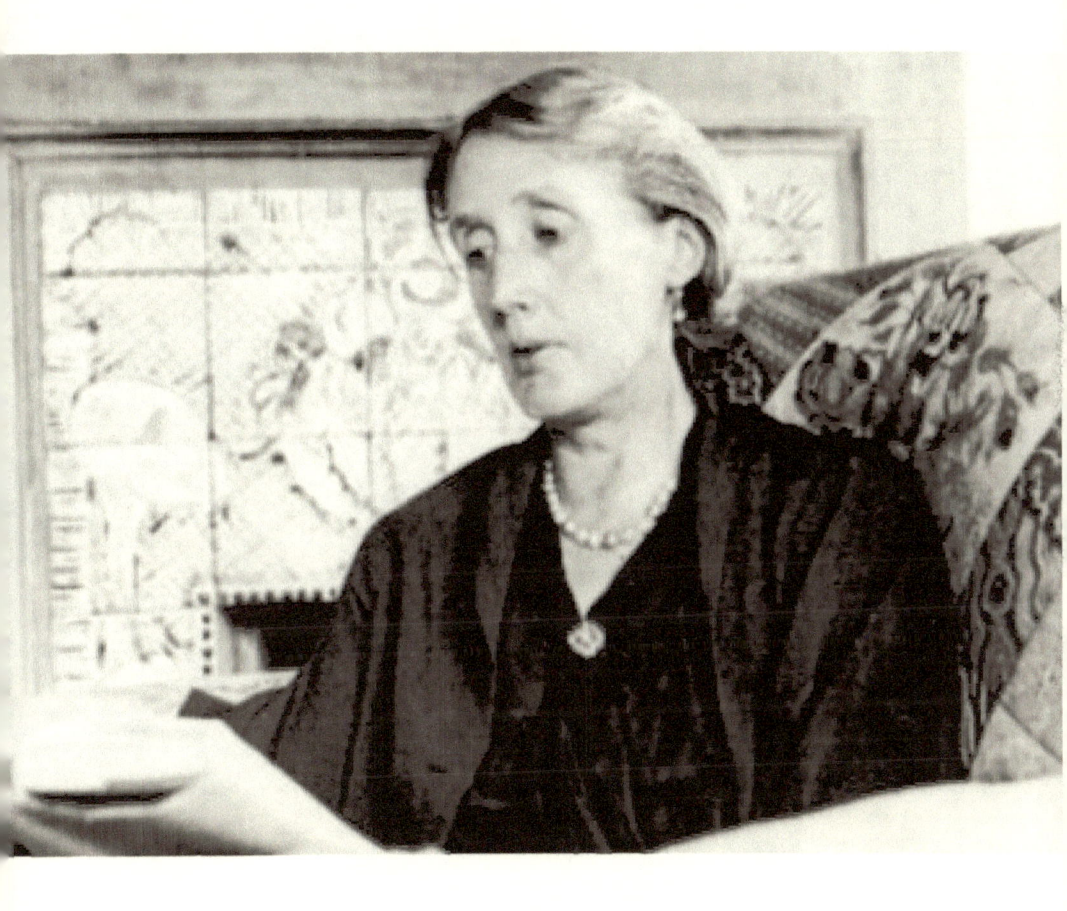

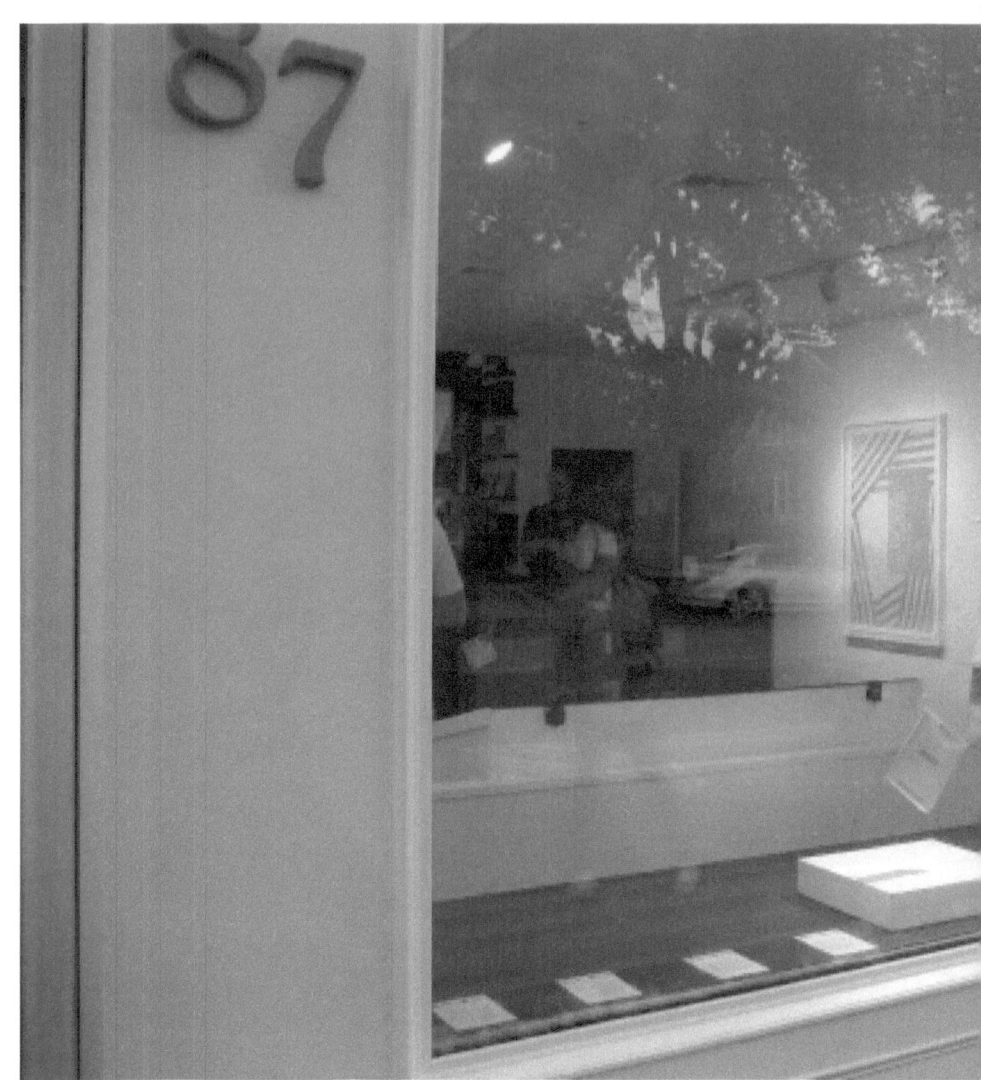

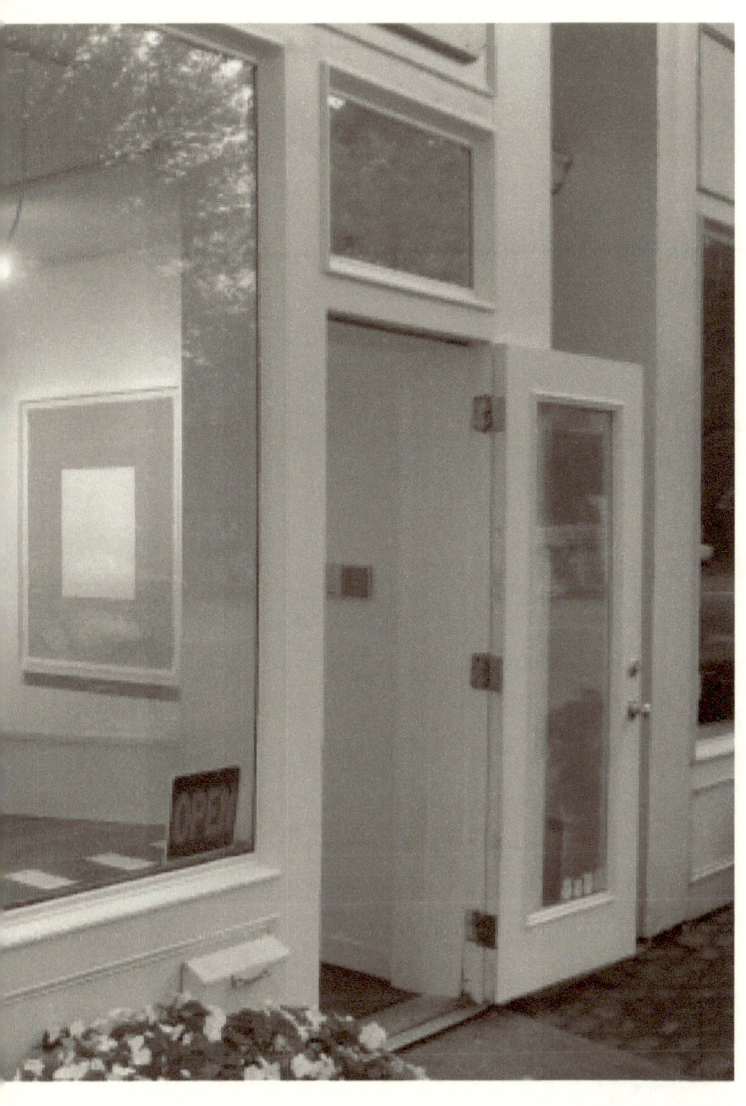

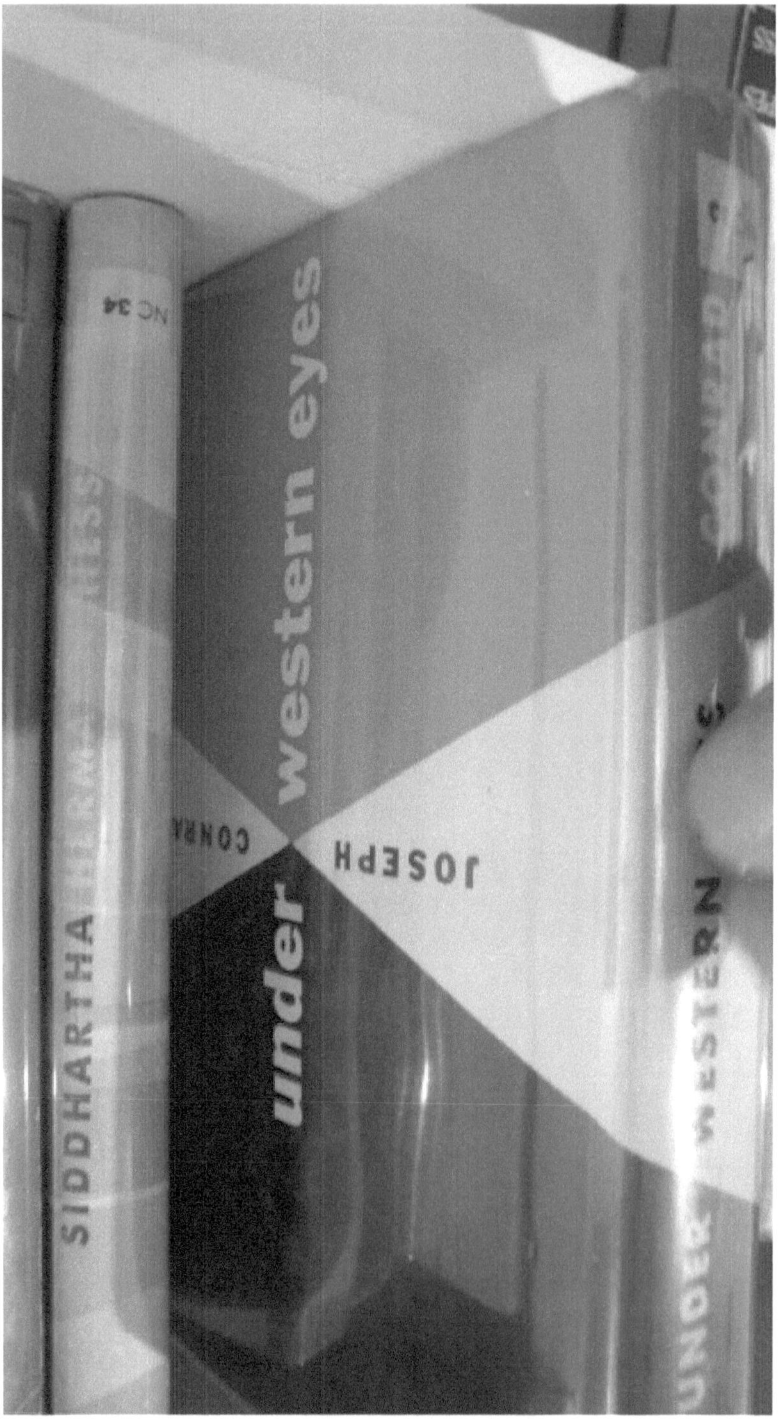

under western eyes

JOSEPH

CONRAD

SIDDHARTHA HESS

NC 34

CONRAD

UNDER WESTERN

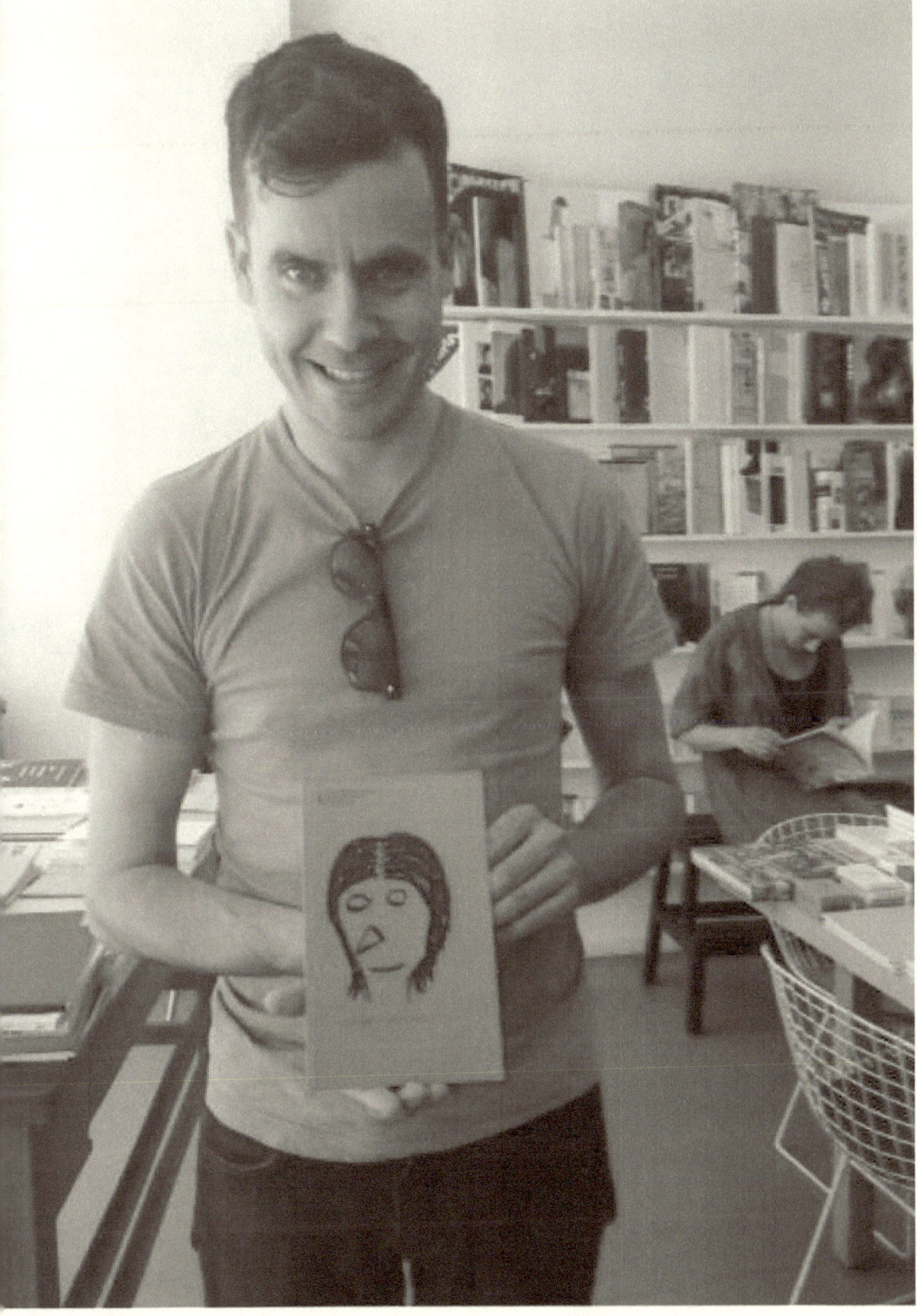

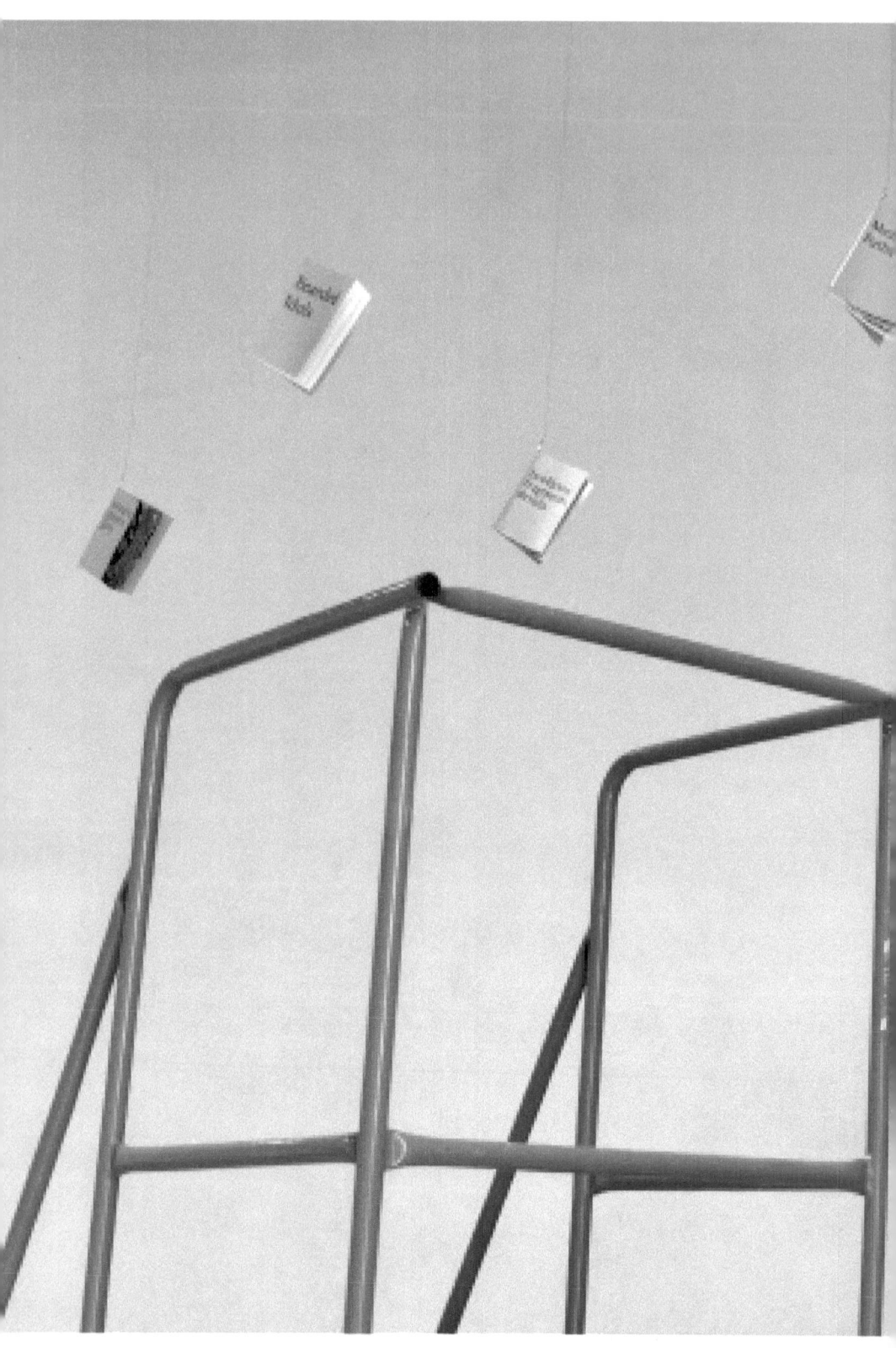

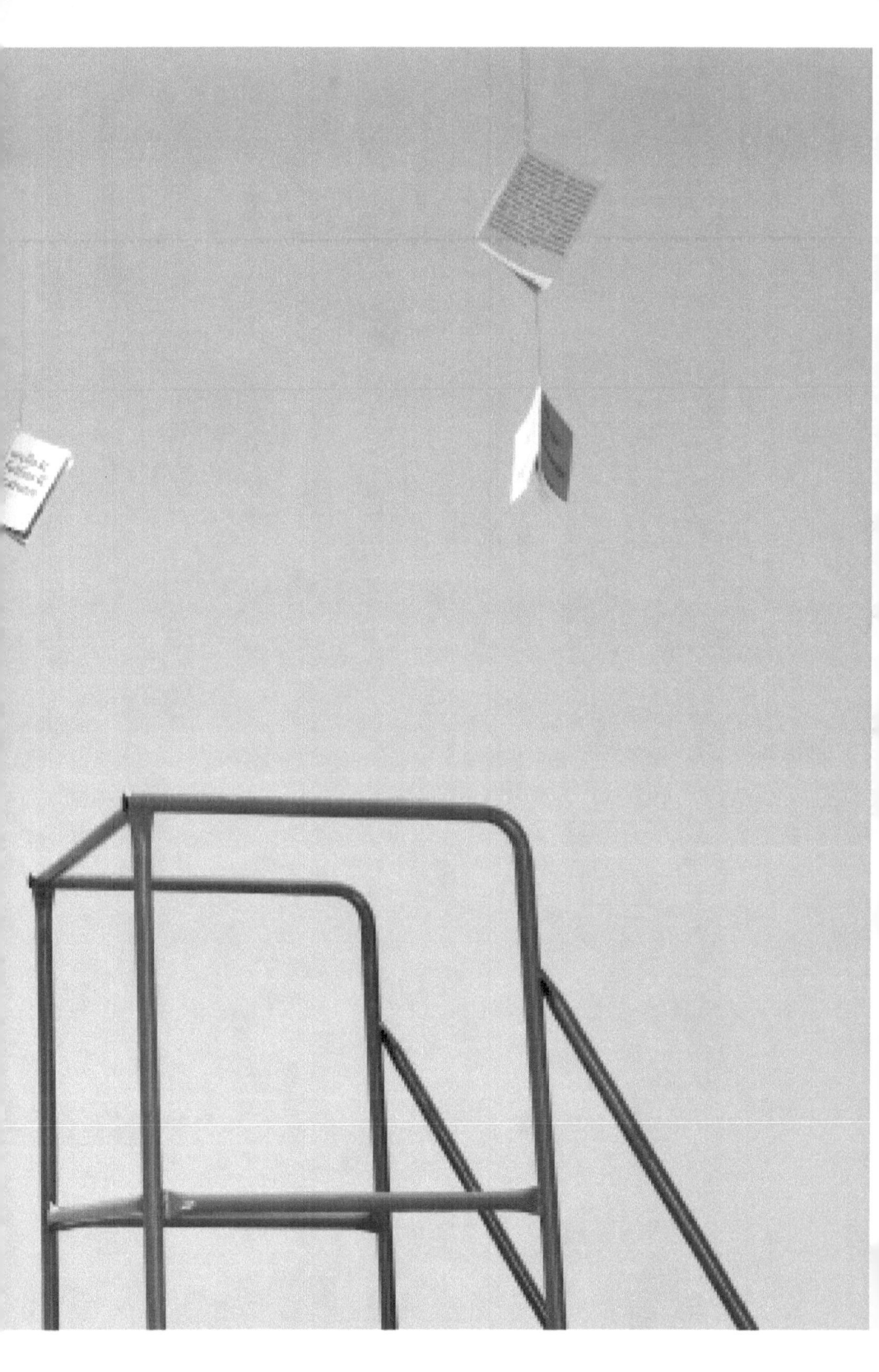

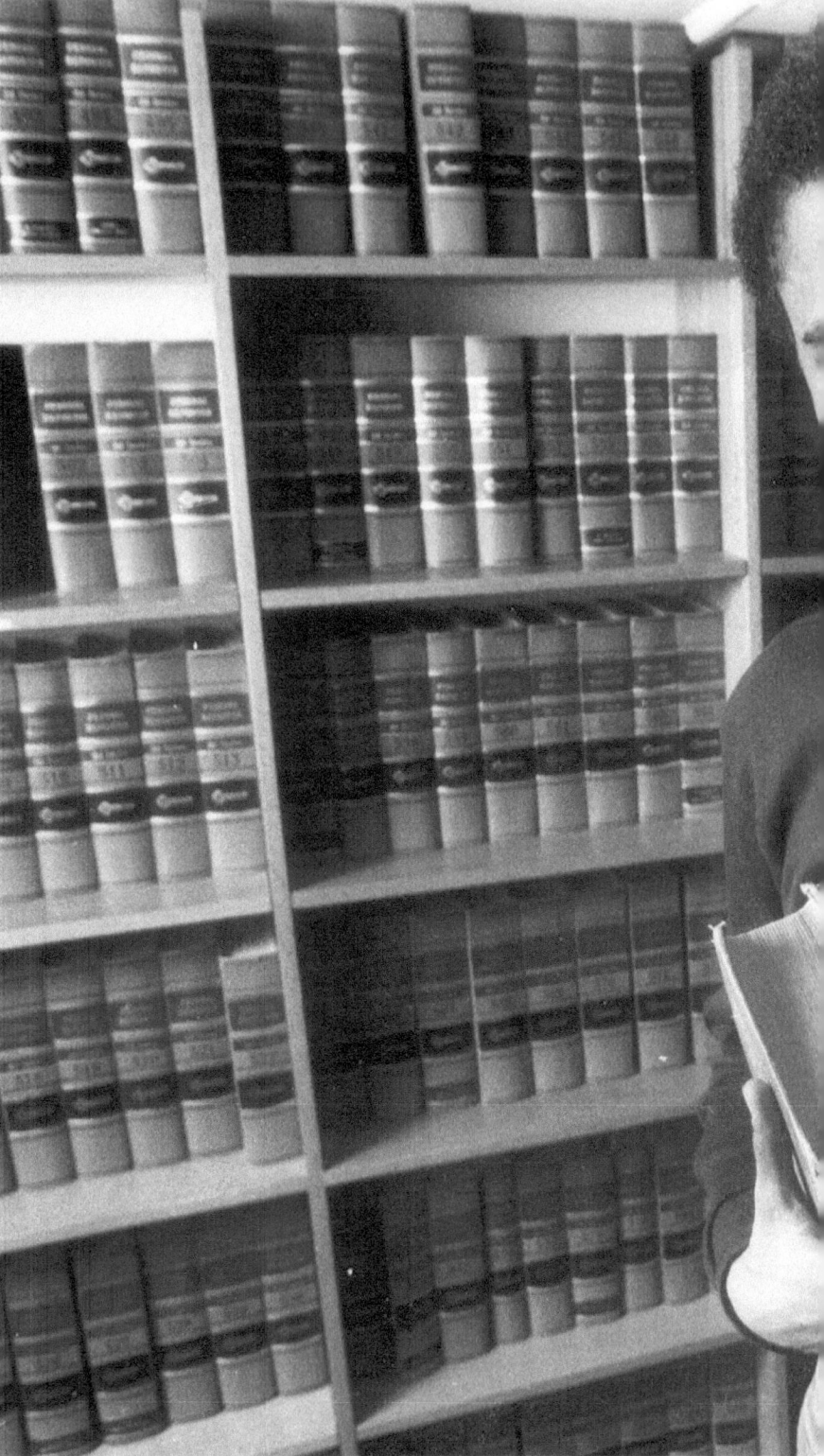

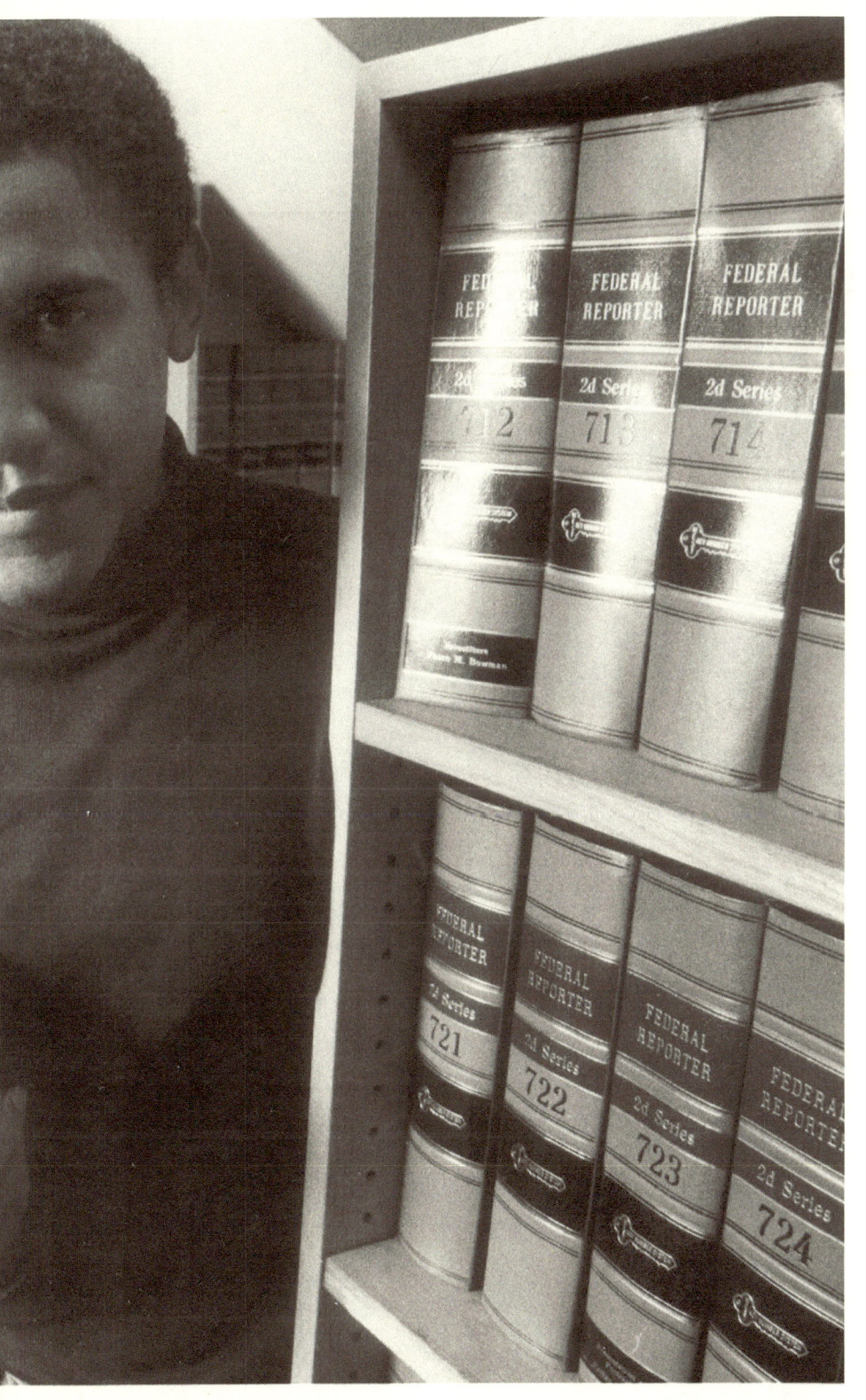

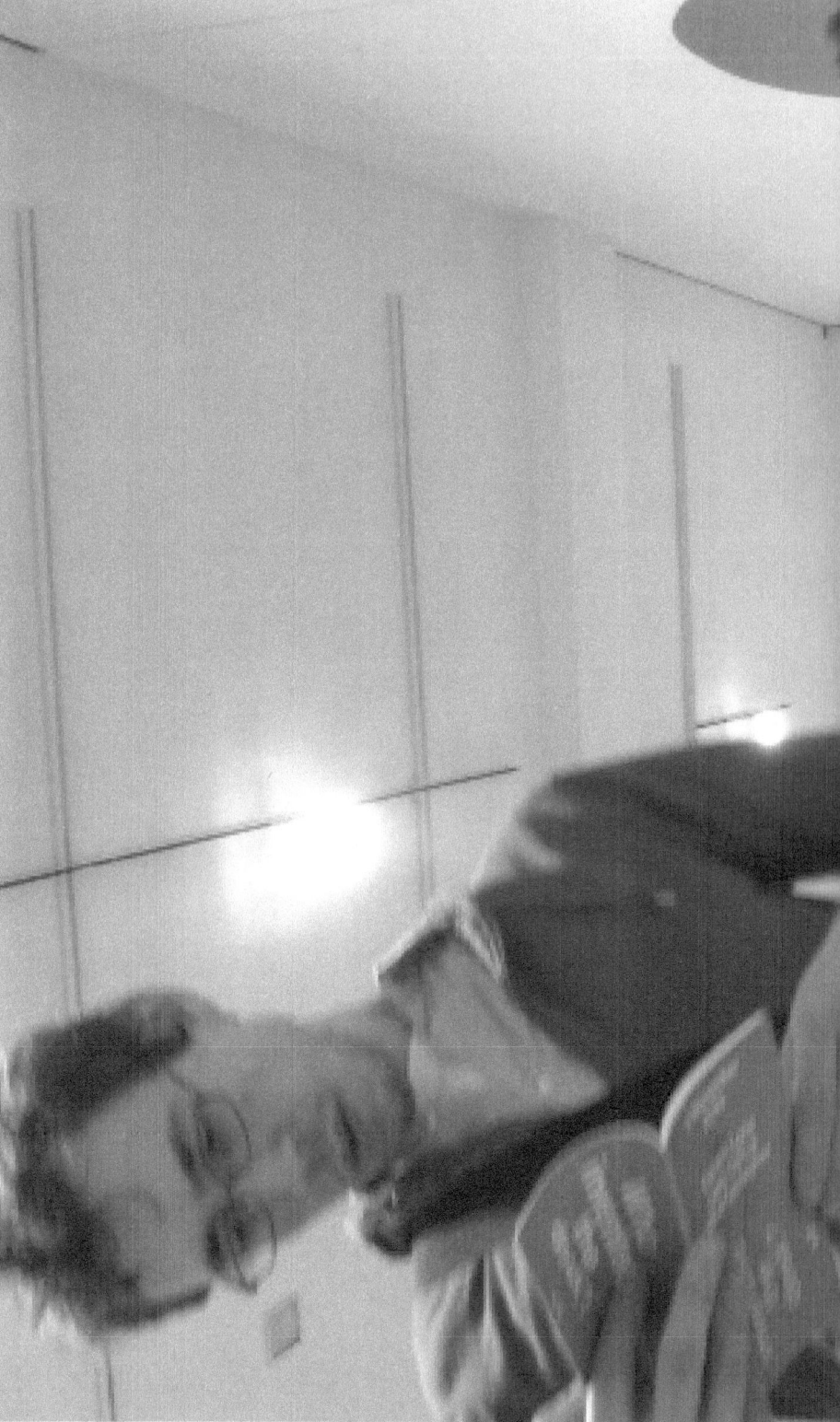

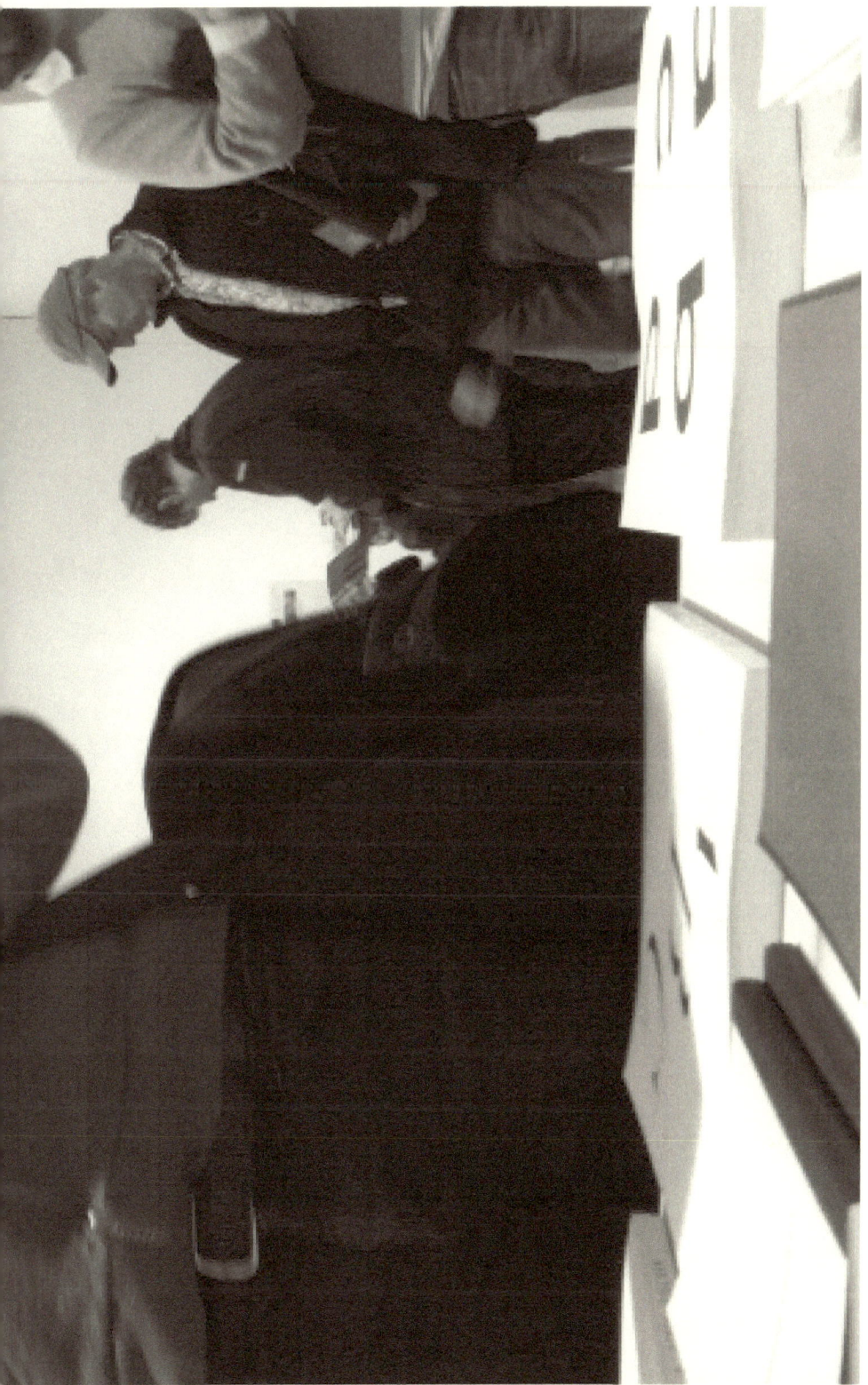

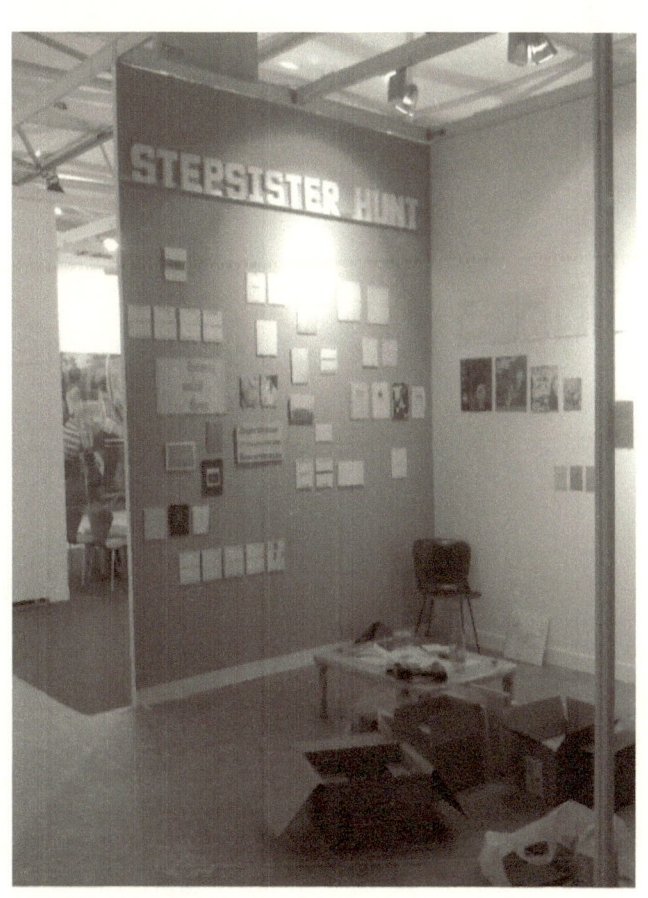

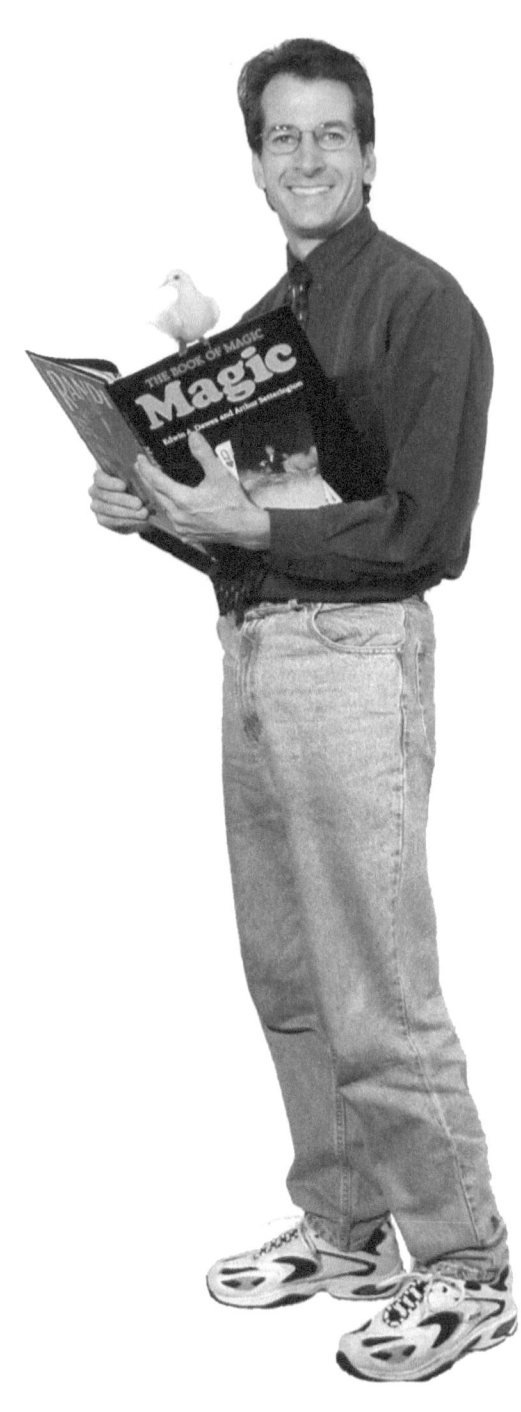

Verlag der Buchhandlung Walther König

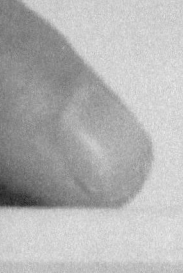

Kippenberger
Psychobuildings

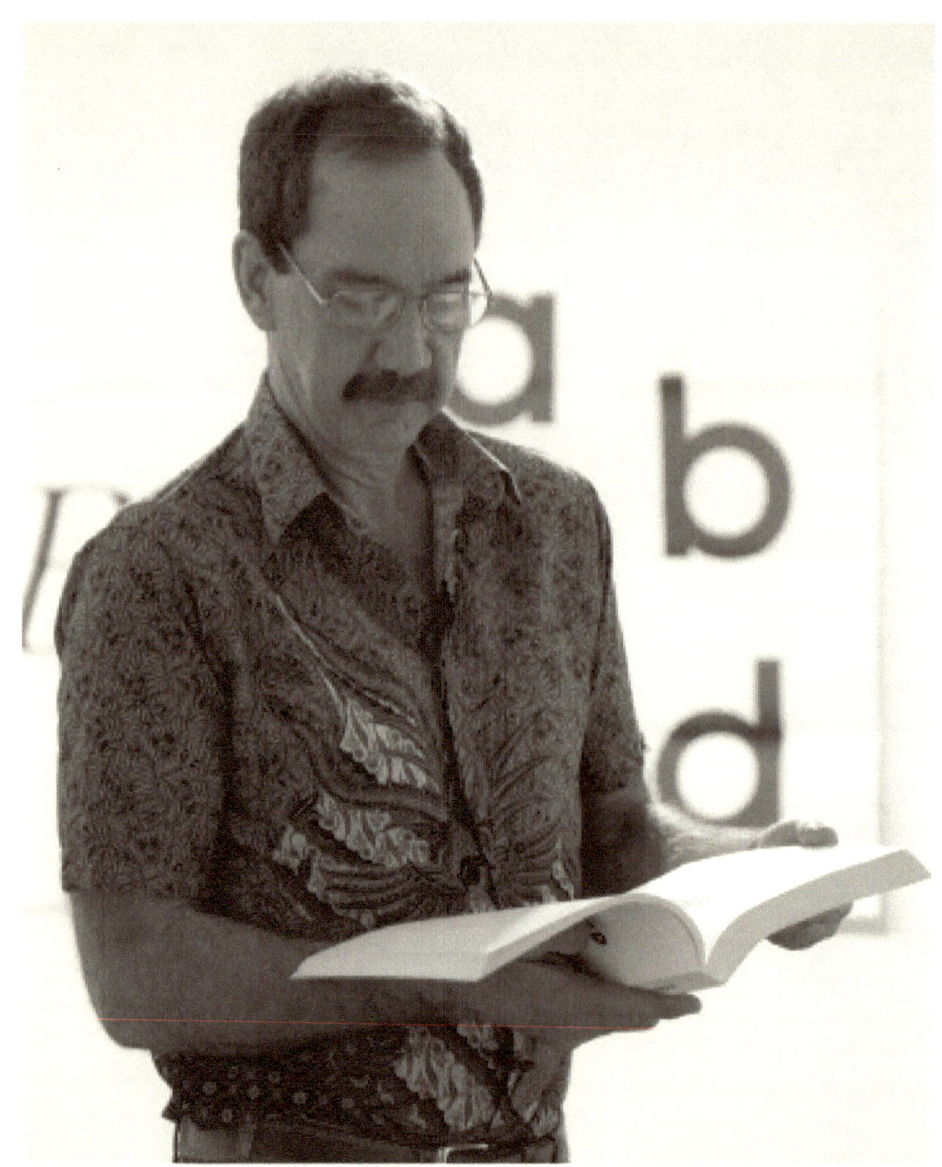

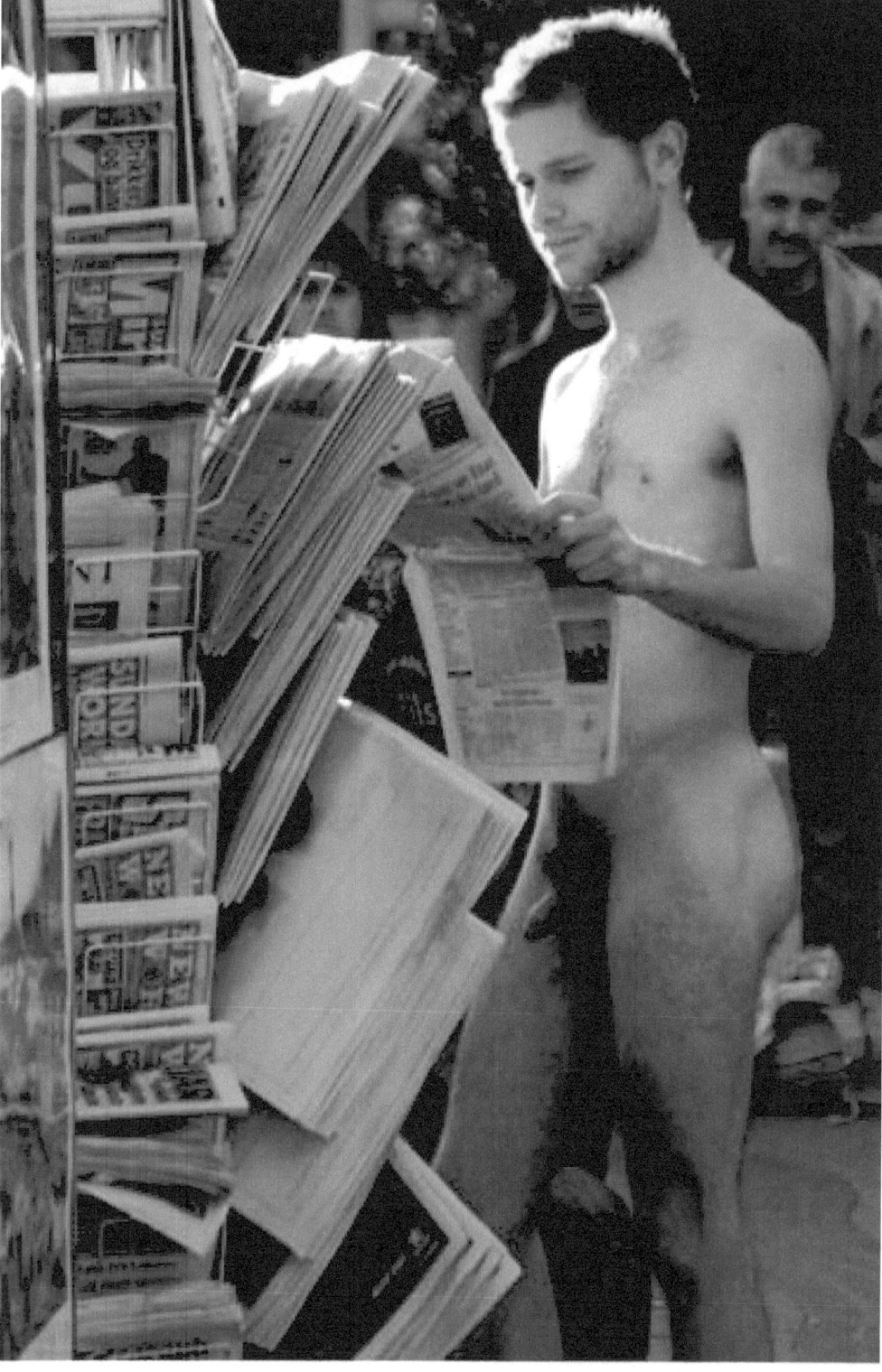

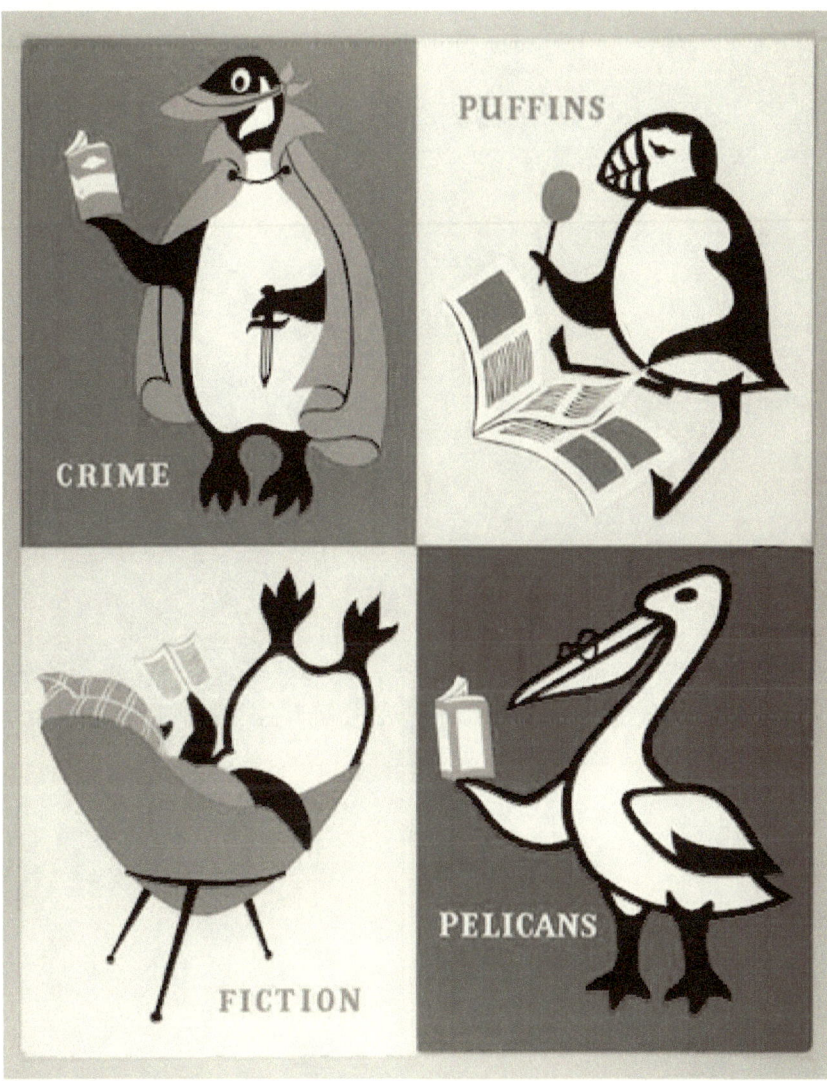

CRIME

PUFFINS

FICTION

PELICANS

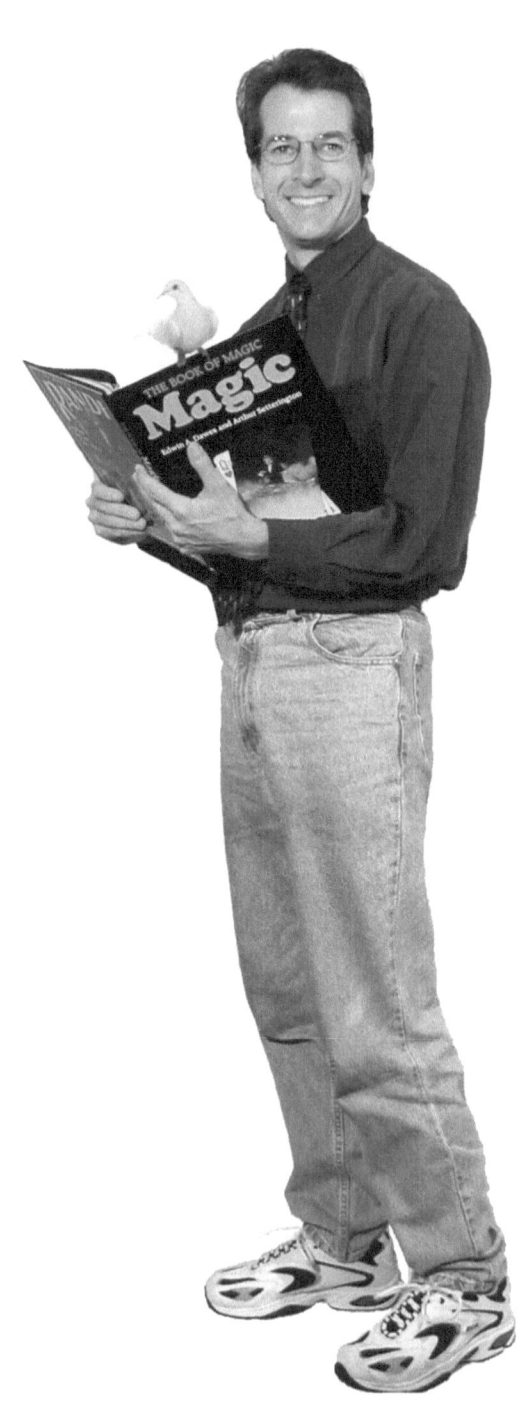

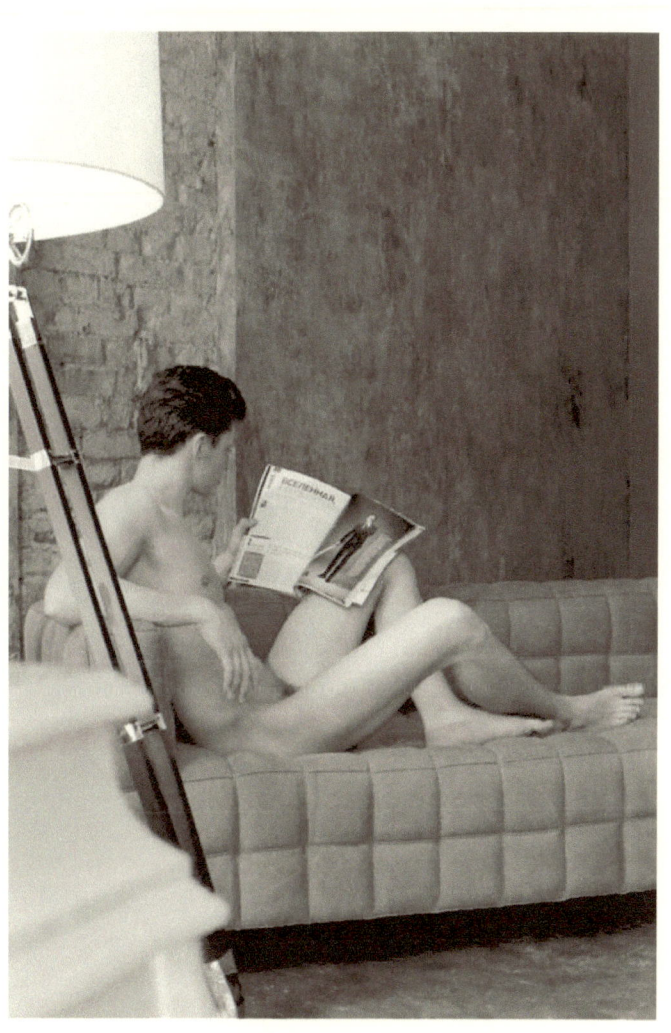

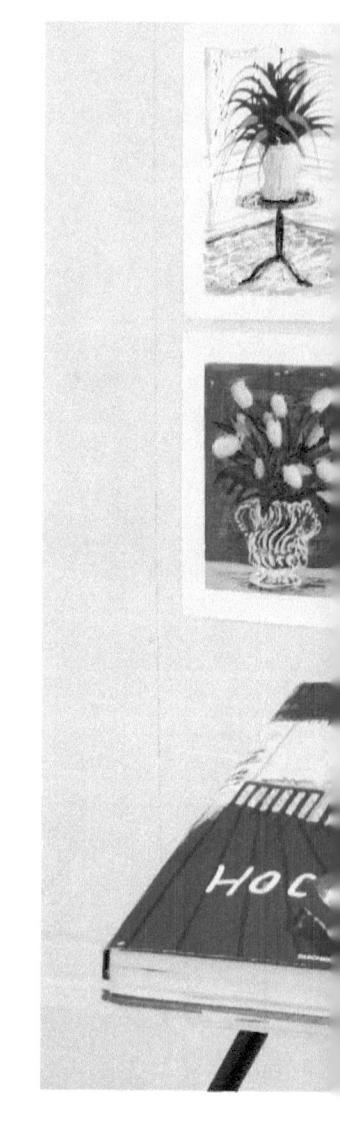

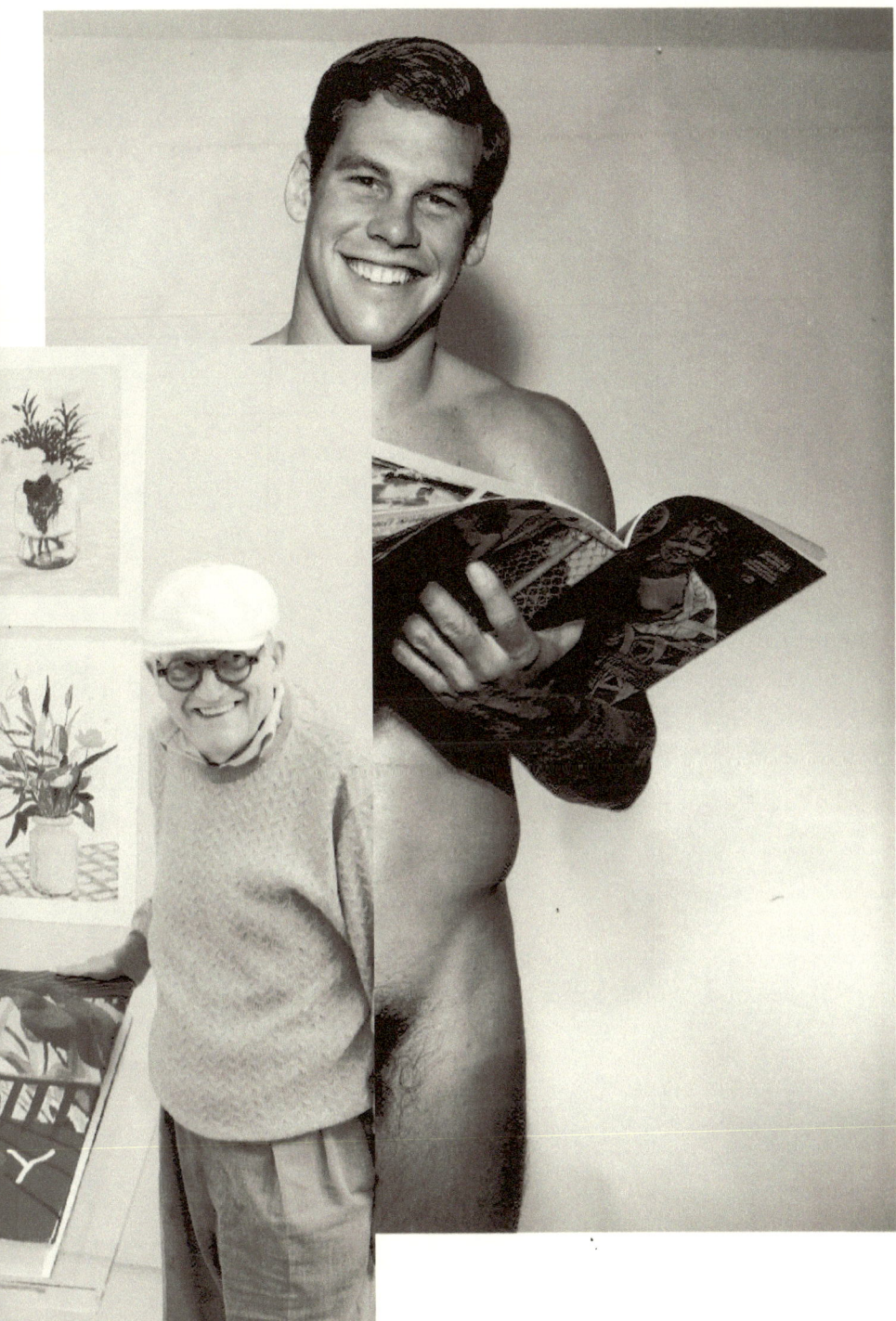

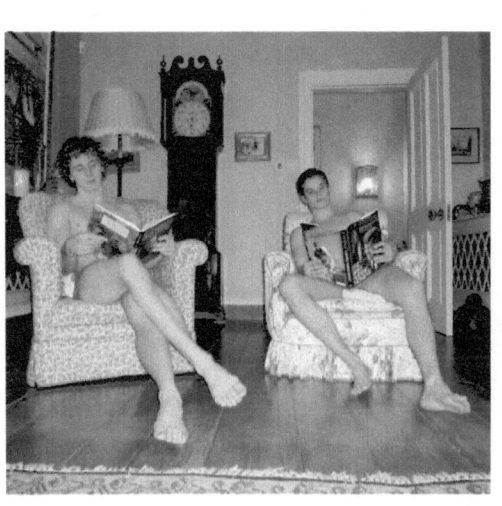

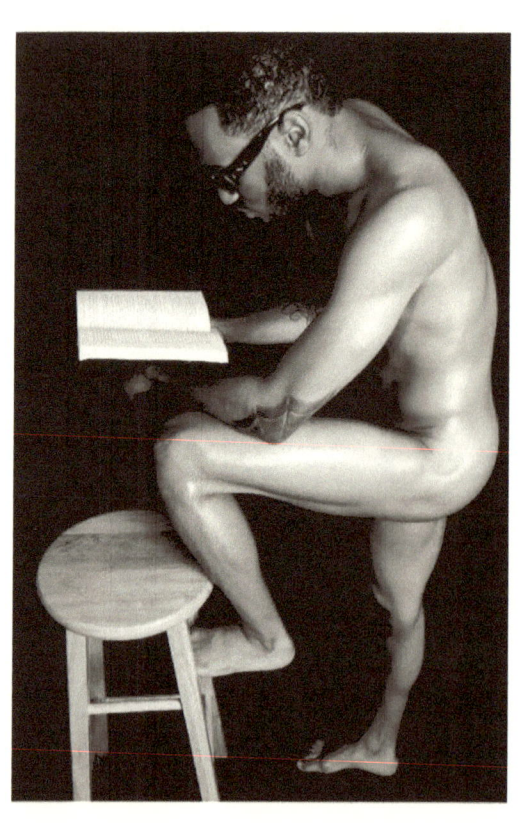

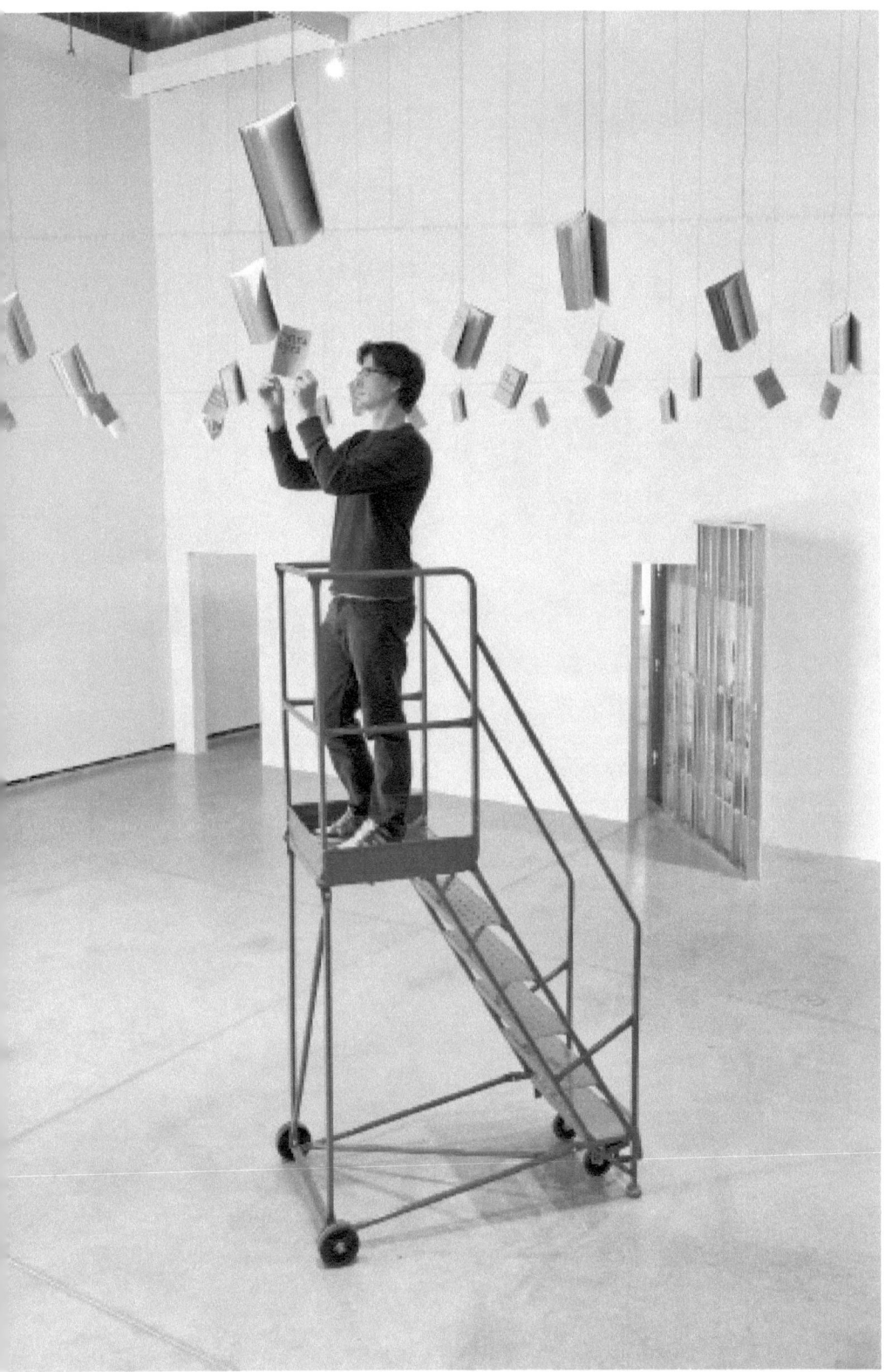

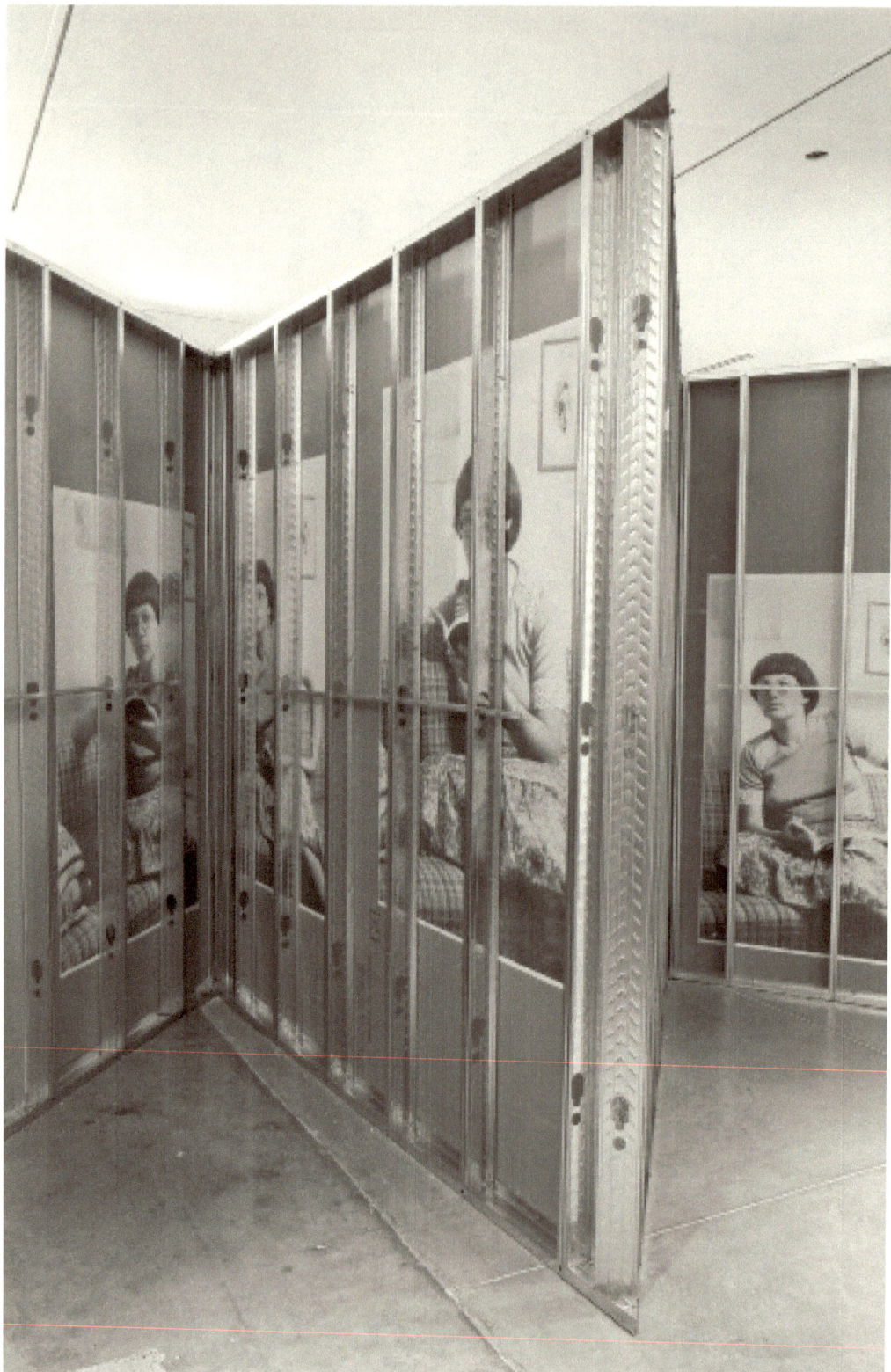

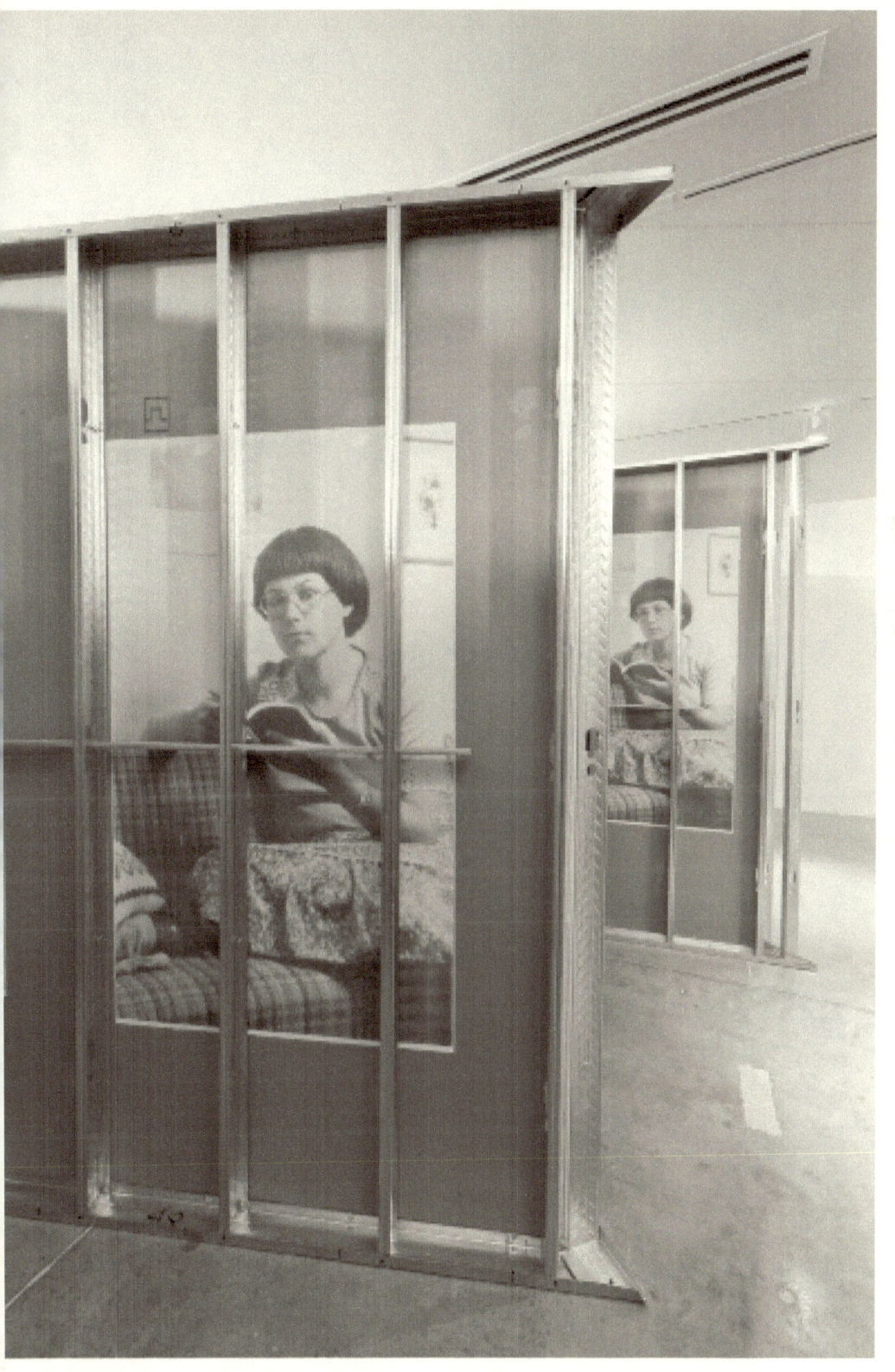

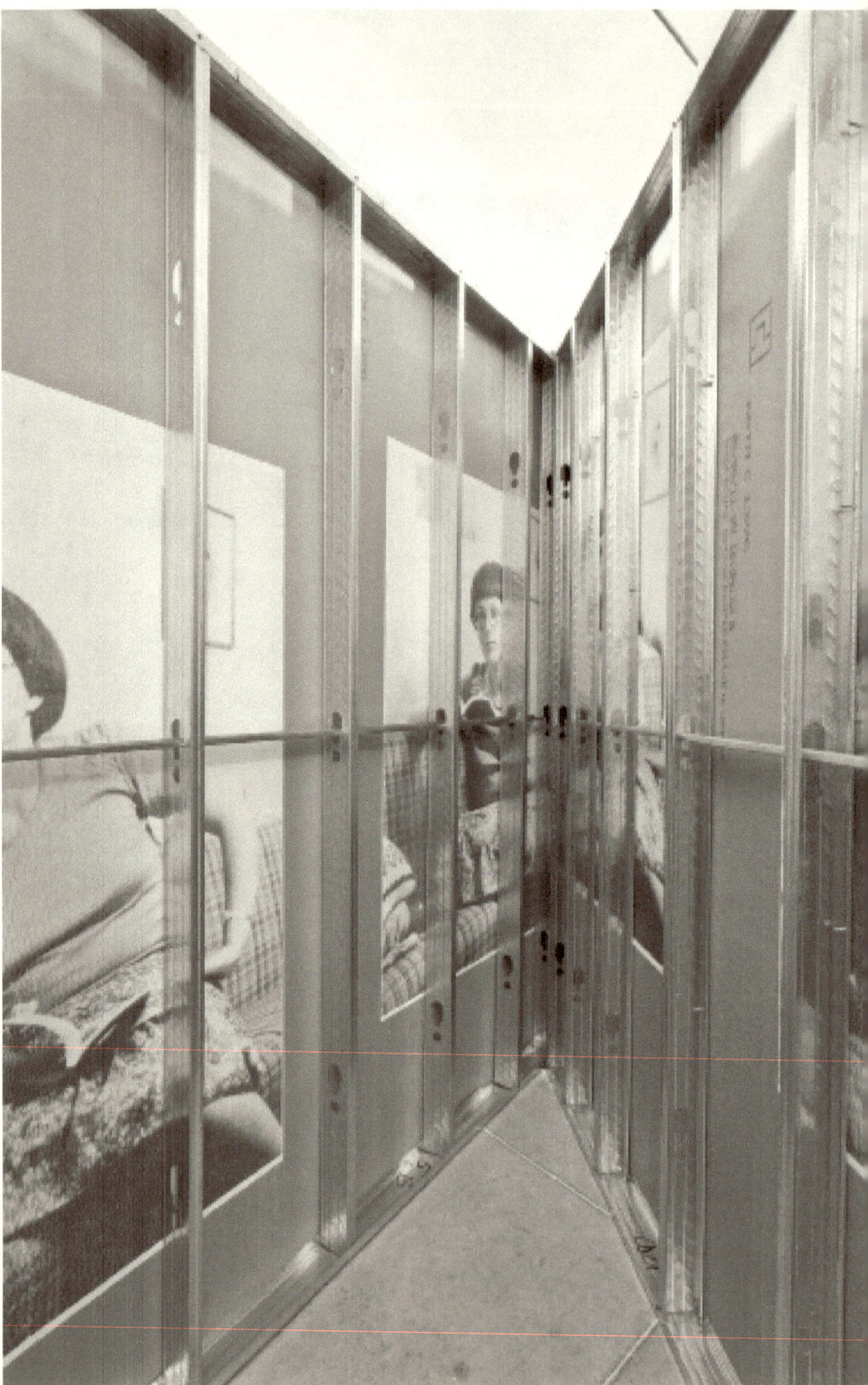

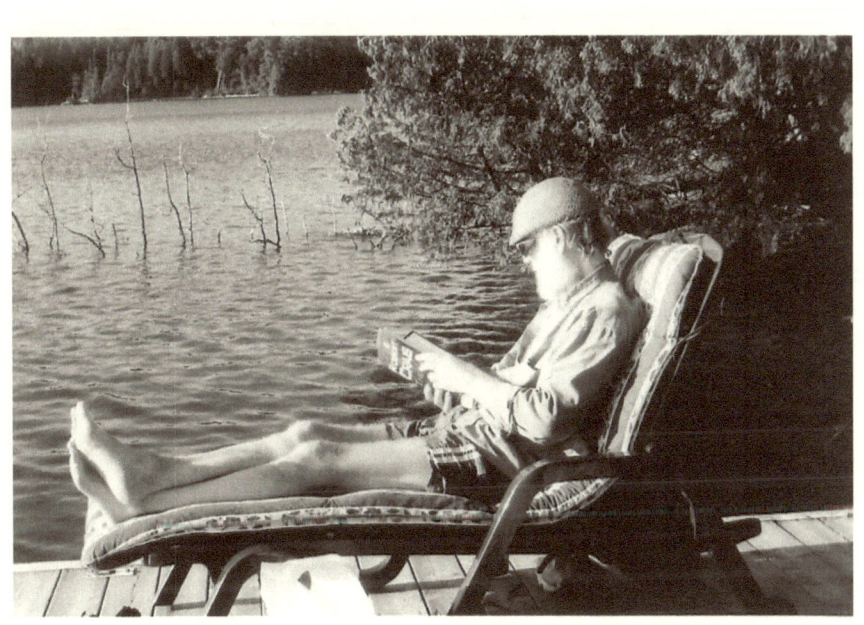

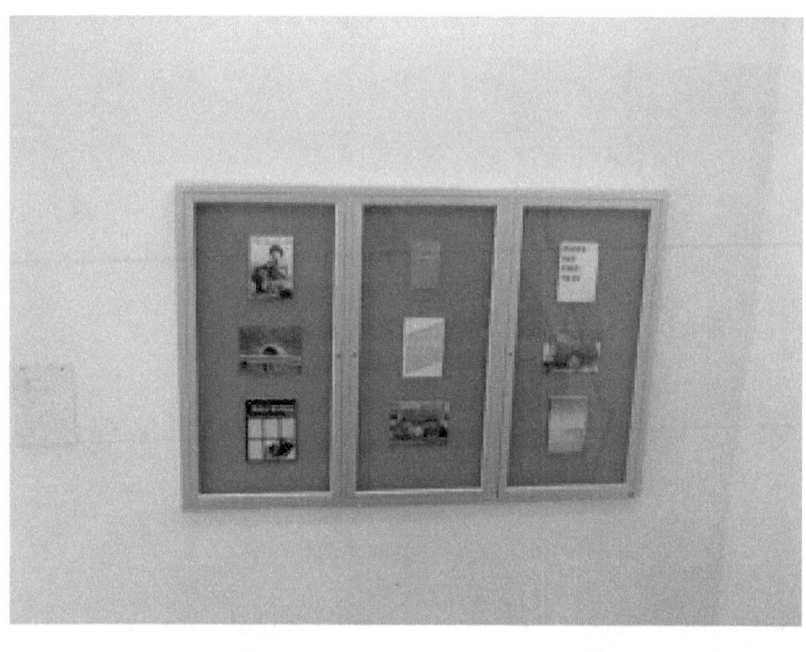

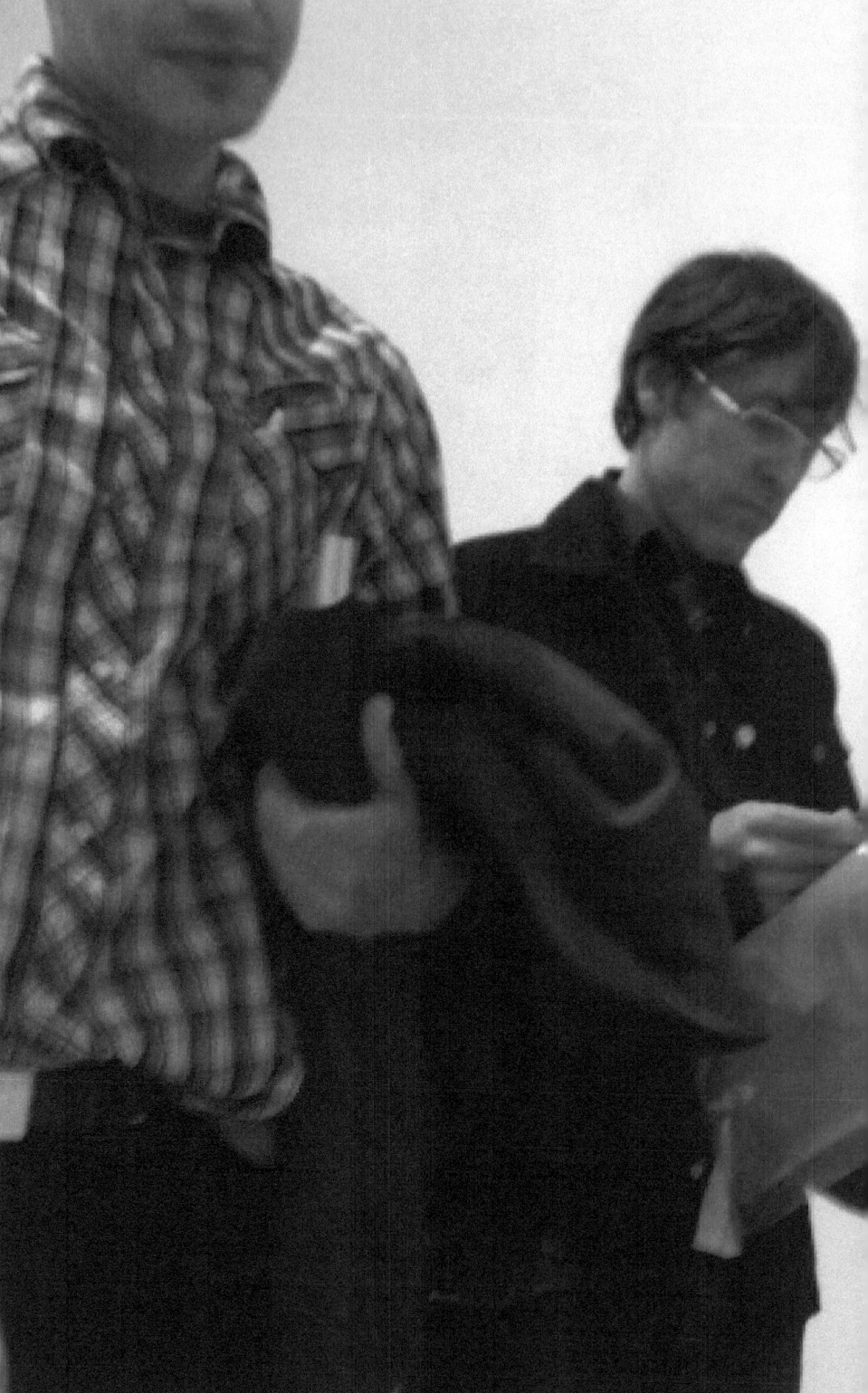

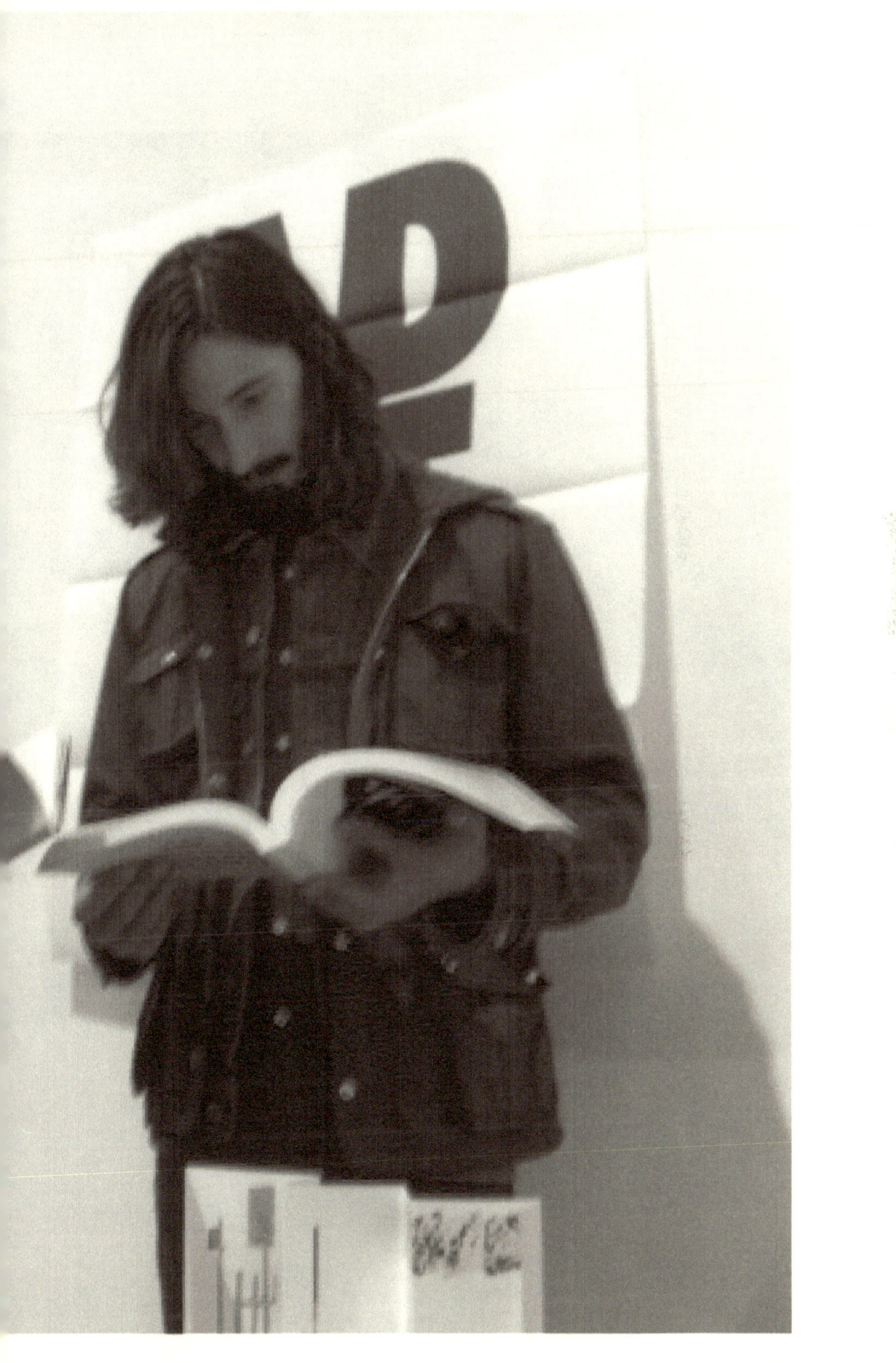

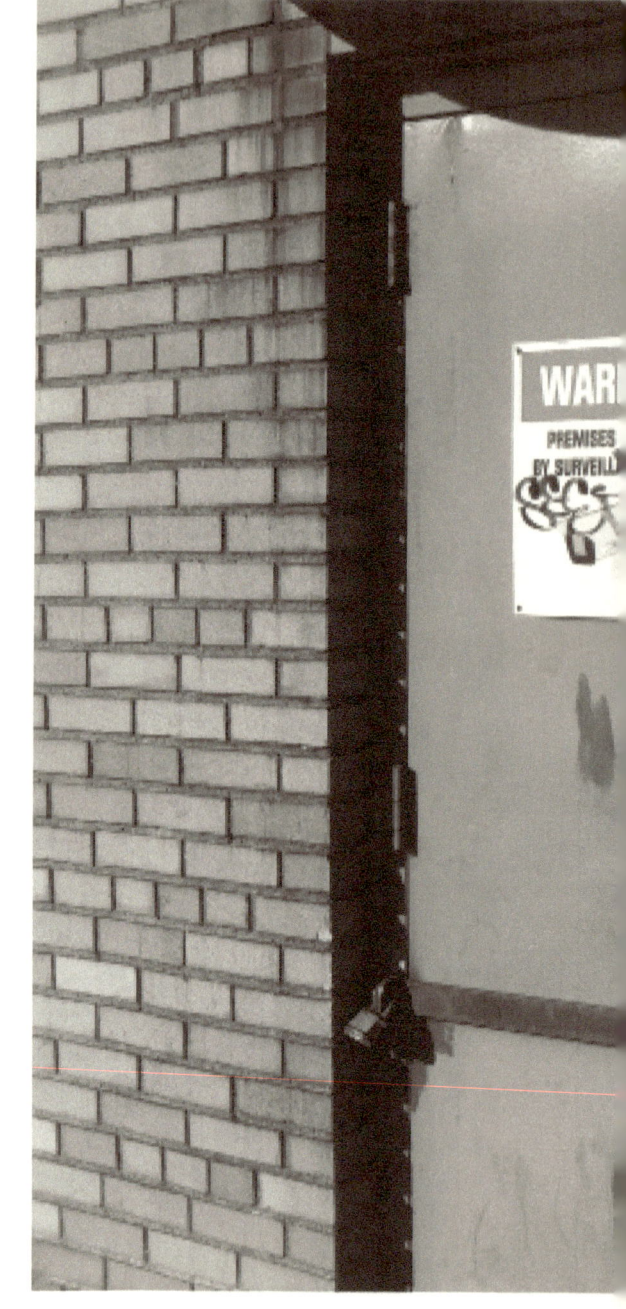

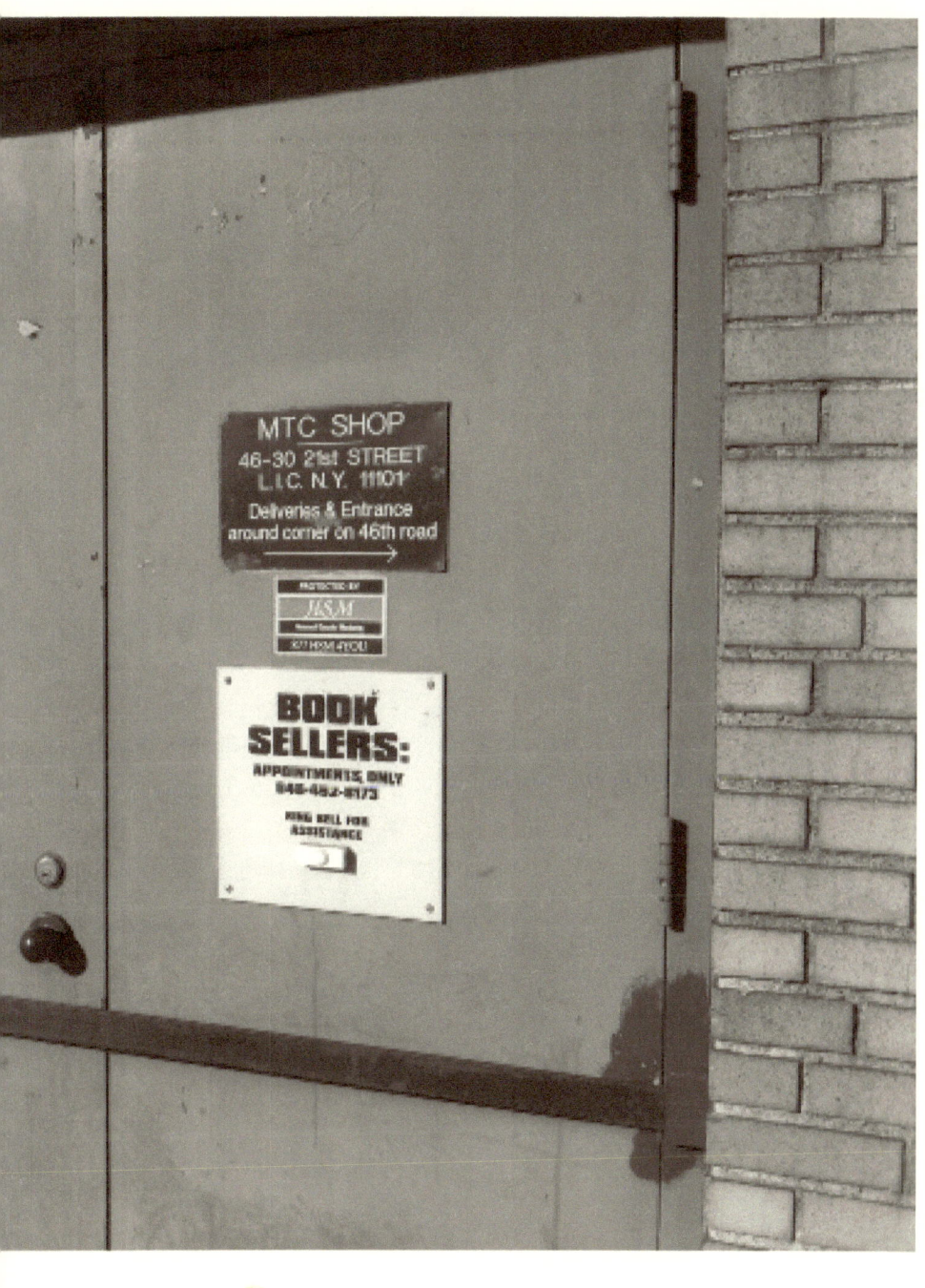

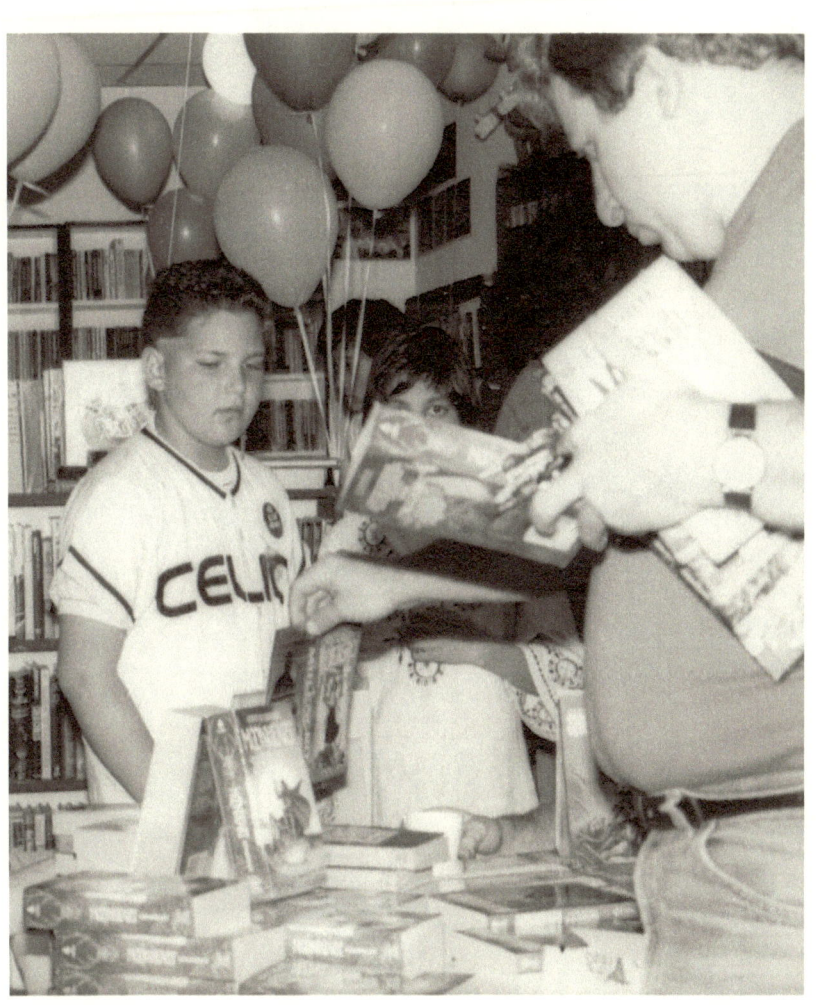

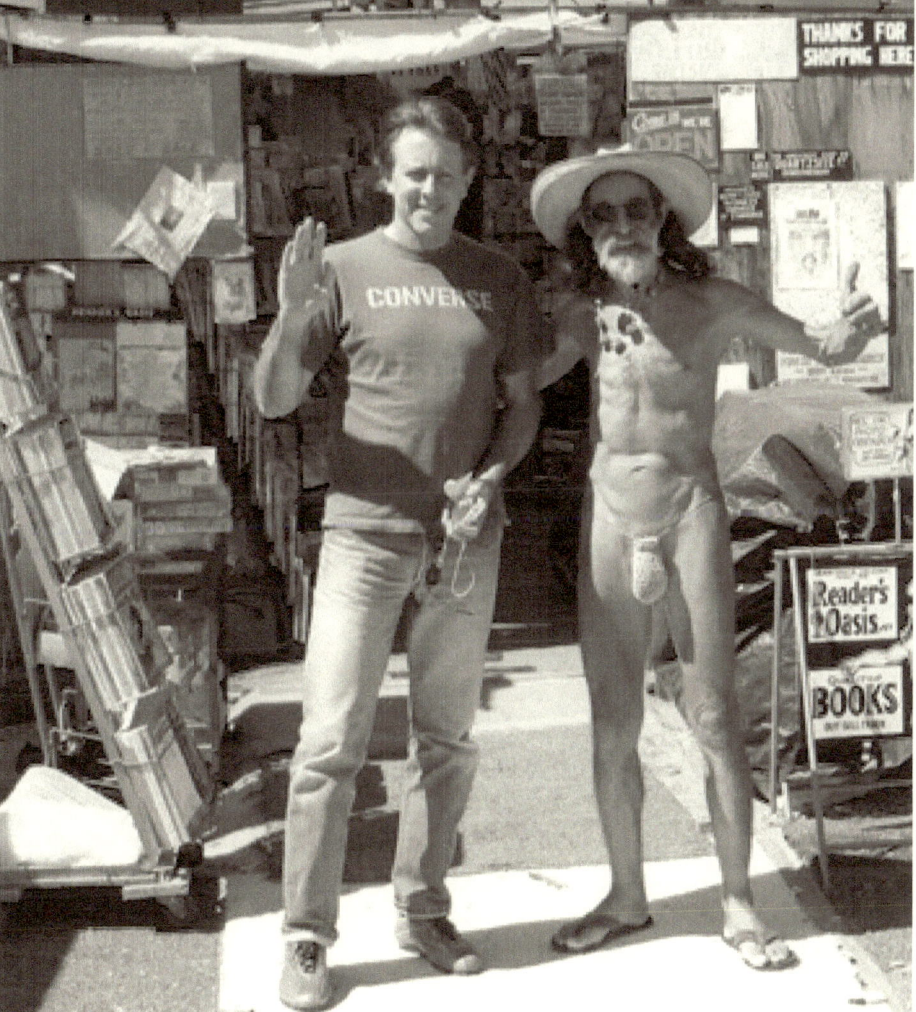

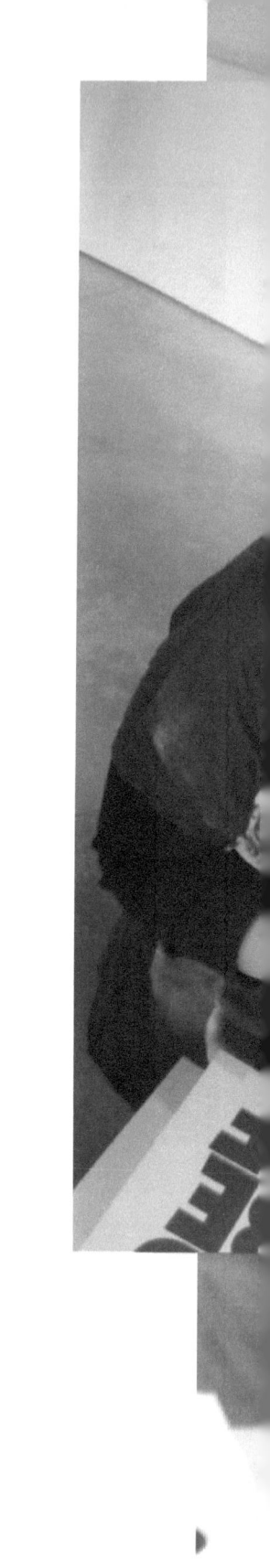

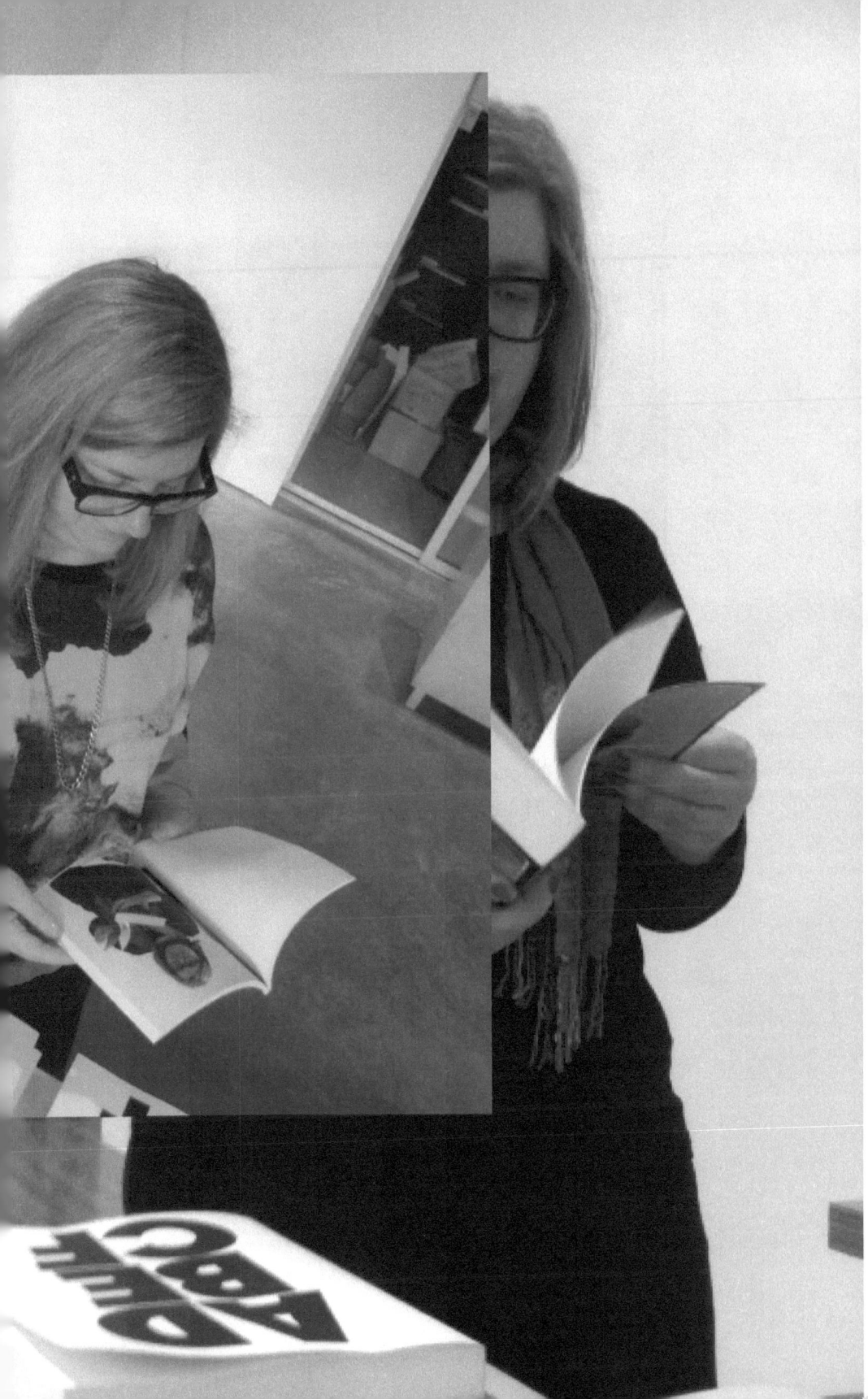

Gulliver's Travels and Other Works

by Jonathan Swift

Edited with an Introduction by

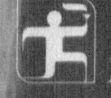

Modern Library College Editions

Gulliver's Travels

JONATHAN SWIFT

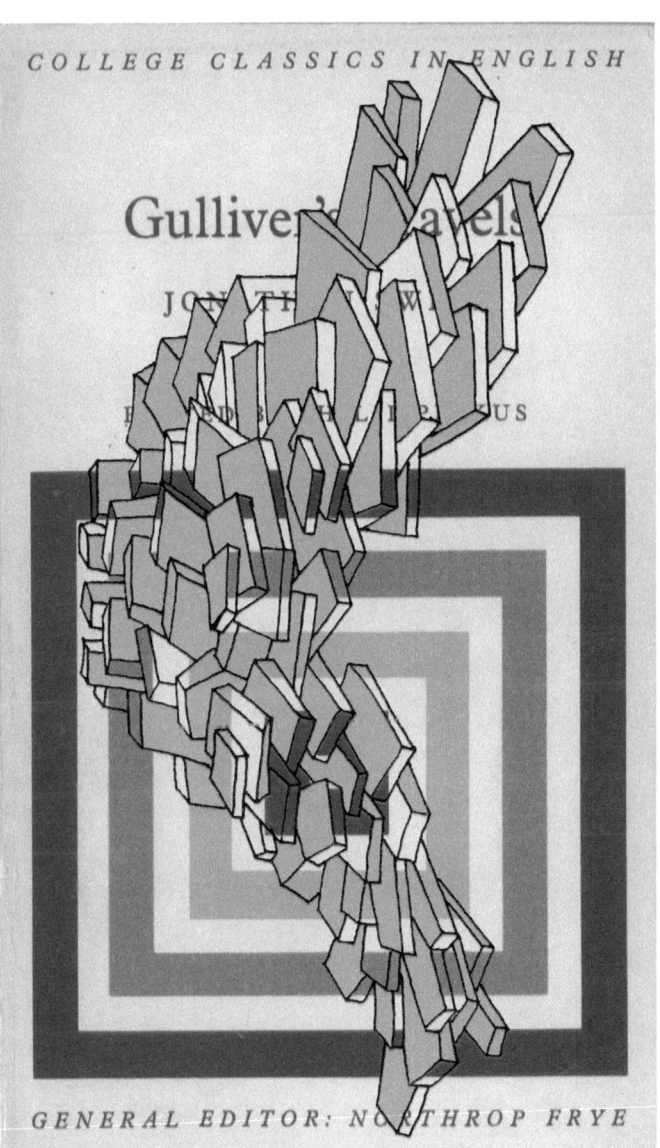

GENERAL EDITOR: NORTHROP FRYE

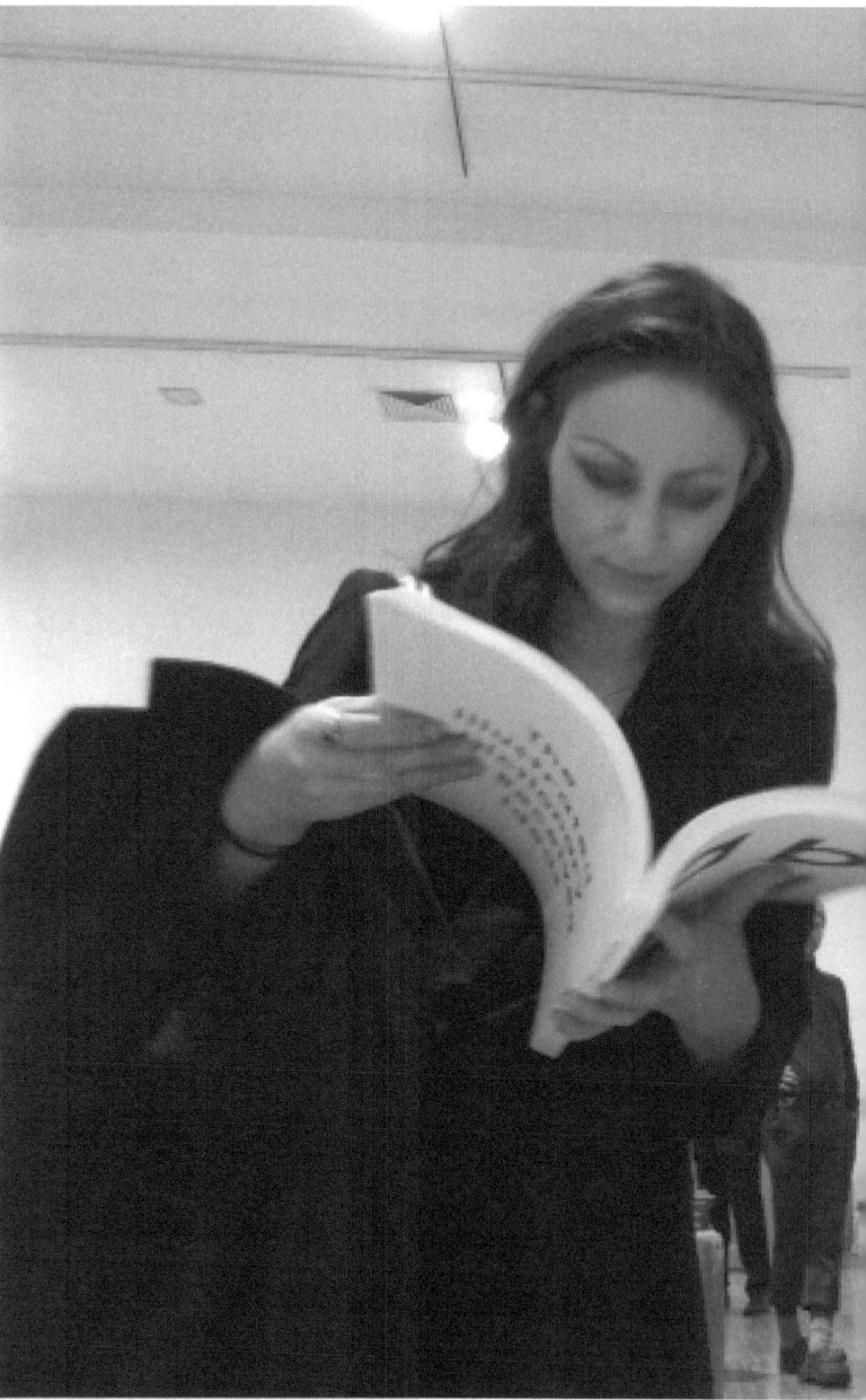

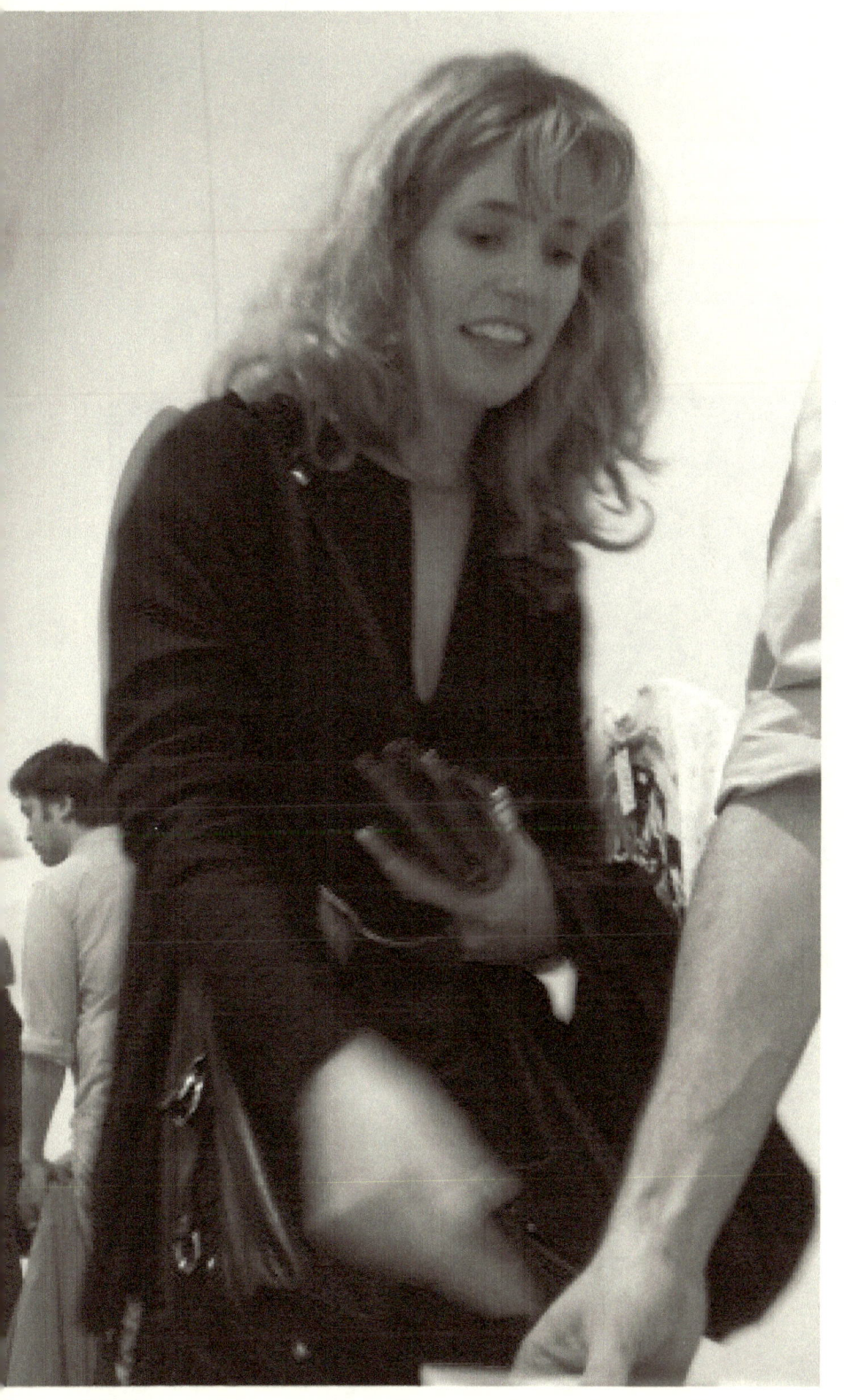

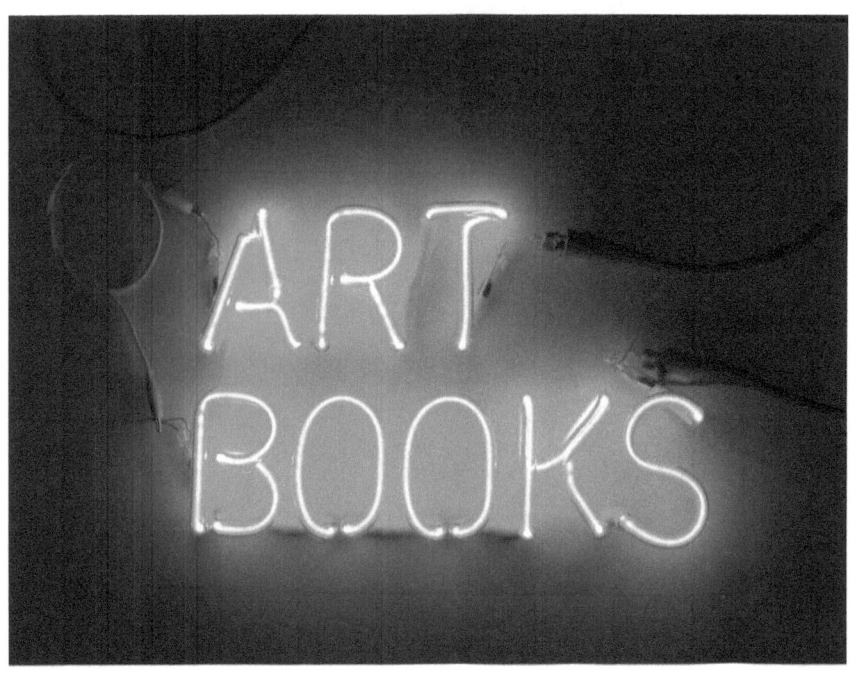

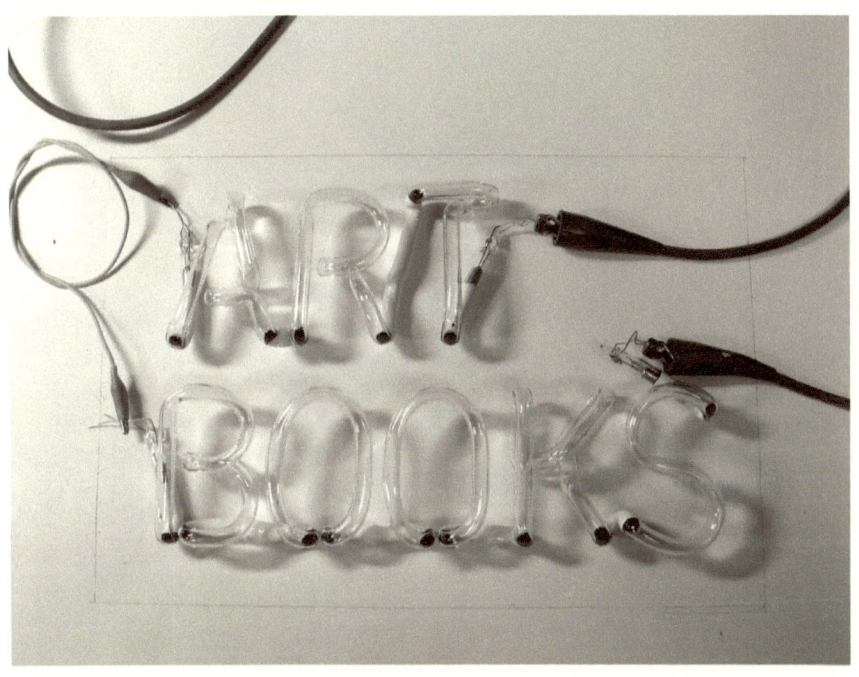

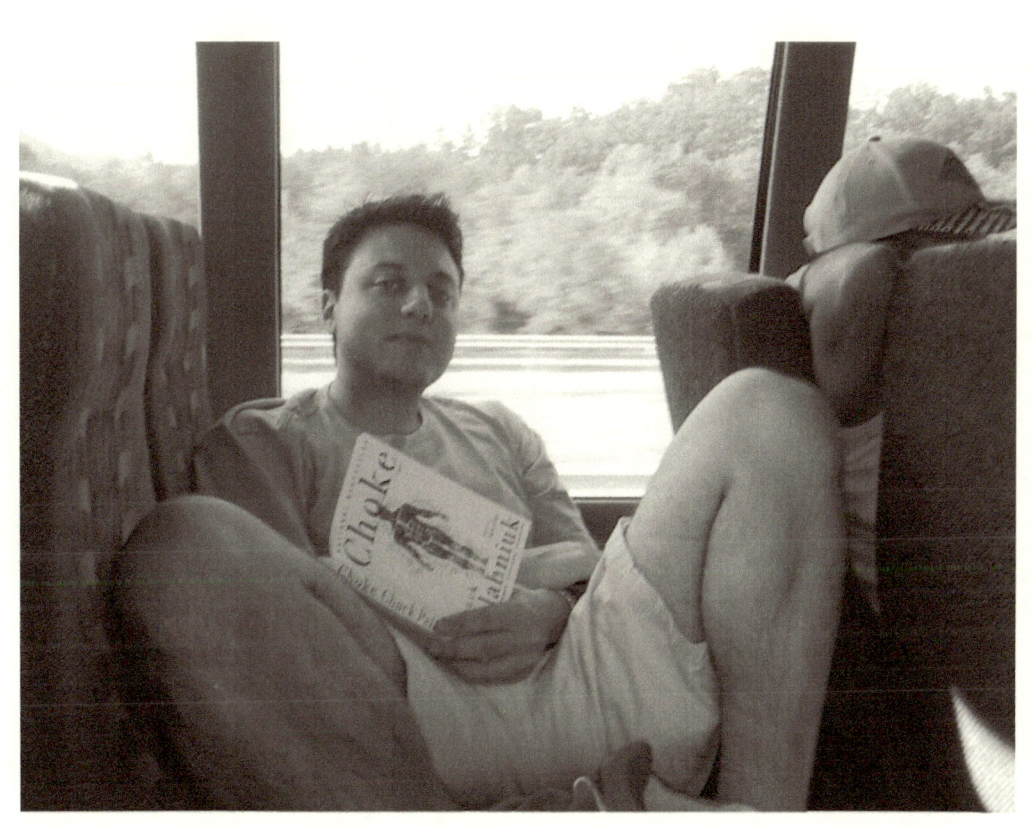

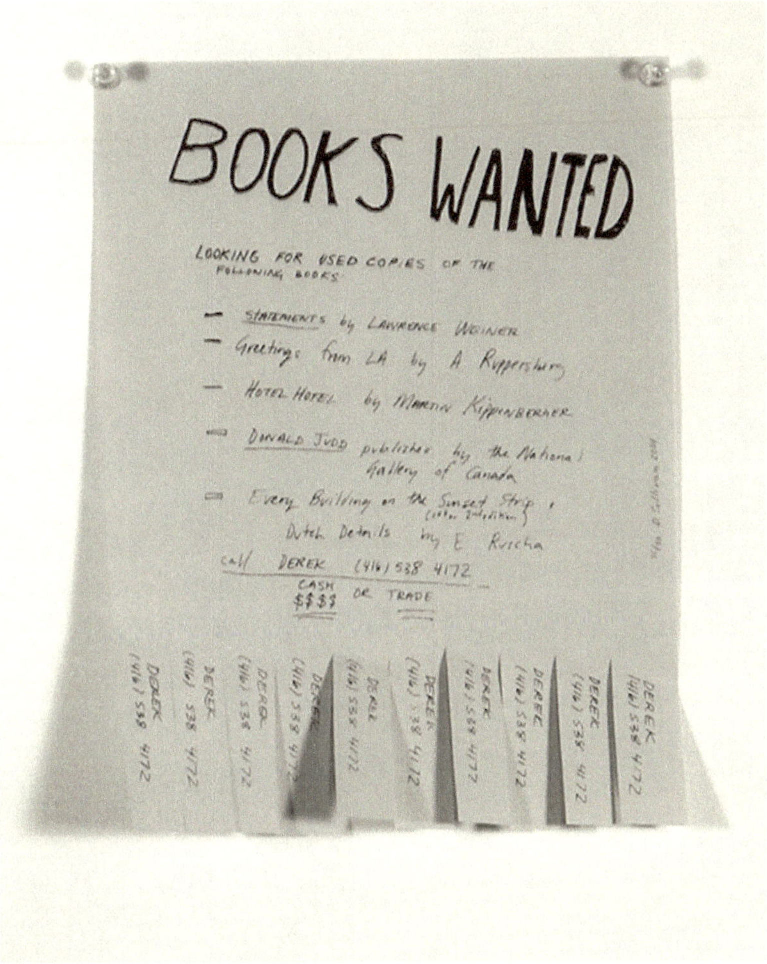
BOOKS WANTED
LOOKING FOR USED COPIES OF THE FOLLOWING BOOKS
— STATEMENTS by LAWRENCE WEINER
— Greetings from LA by A Ruppersberg
— HOTEL HOTEL by MARTIN KIPPENBERGER
— DONALD JUDD published by the National Gallery of Canada
— Every Building on the Sunset Strip + Dutch Details by E Ruscha
call DEREK (416) 538 4172
CASH $$$$ OR TRADE

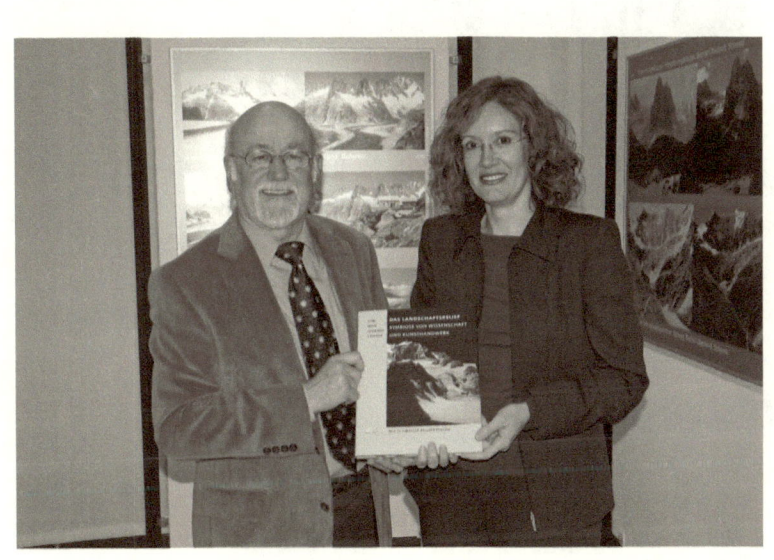

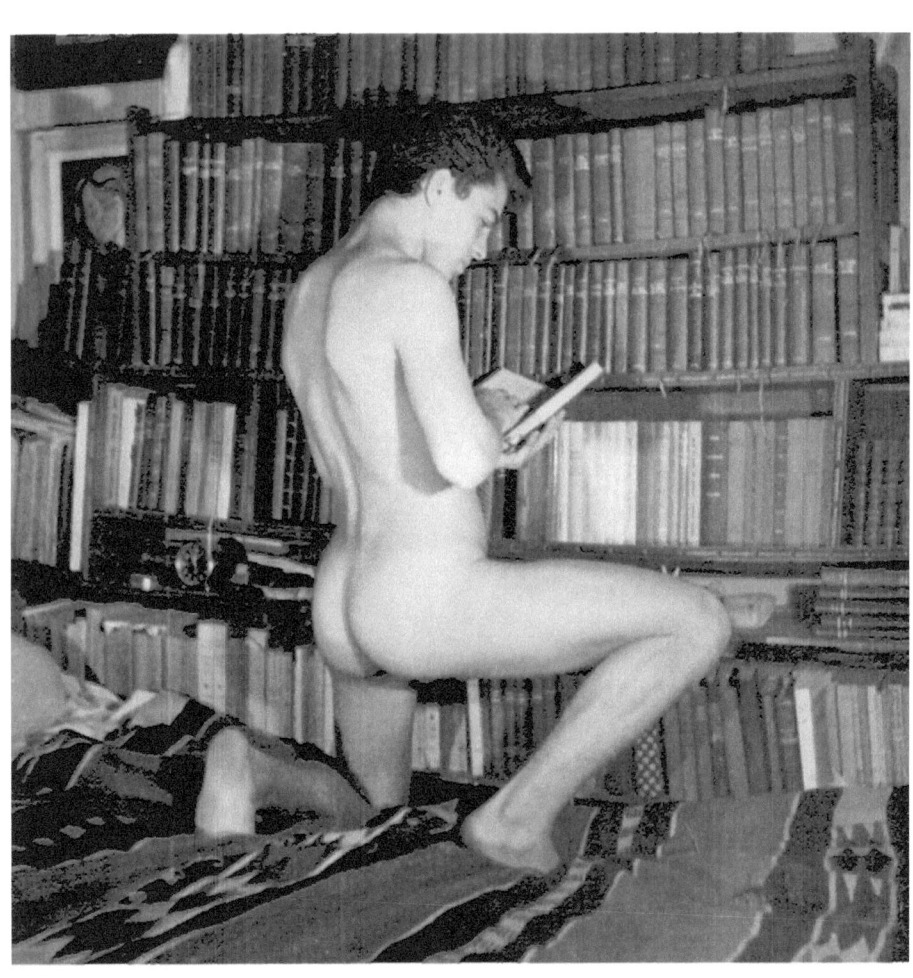

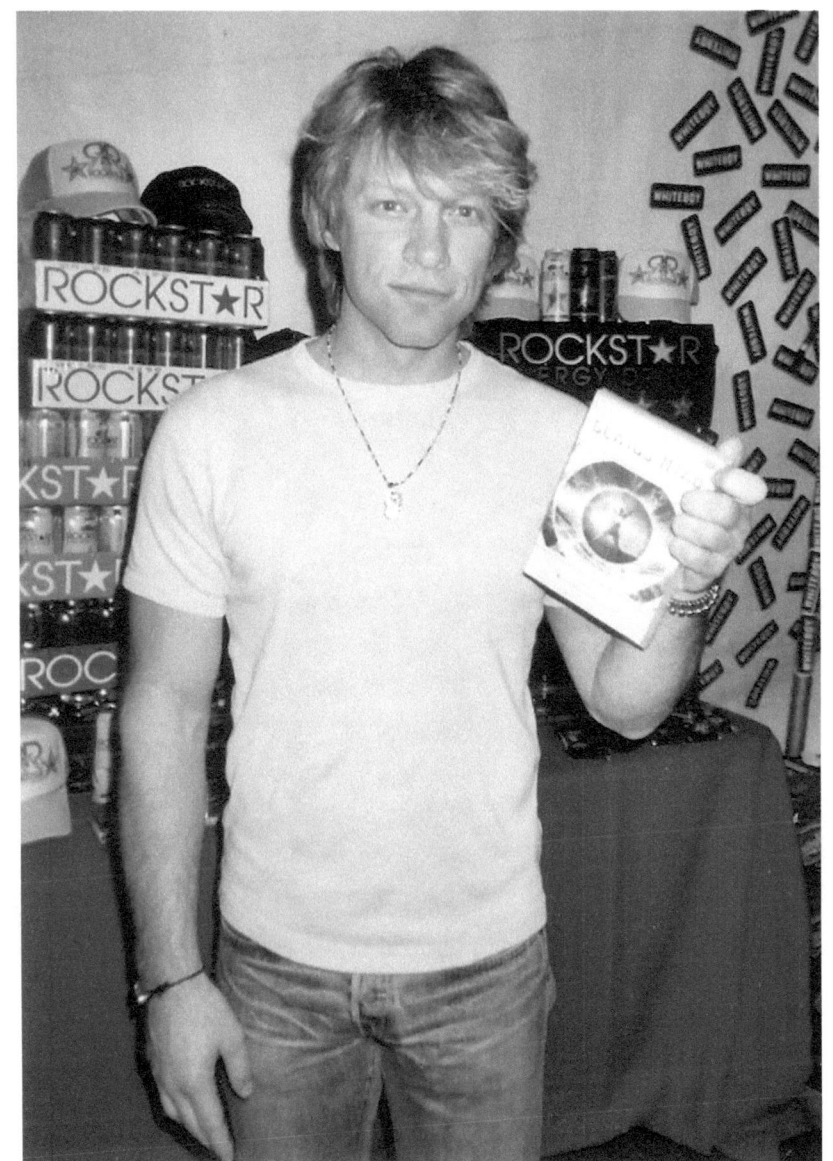

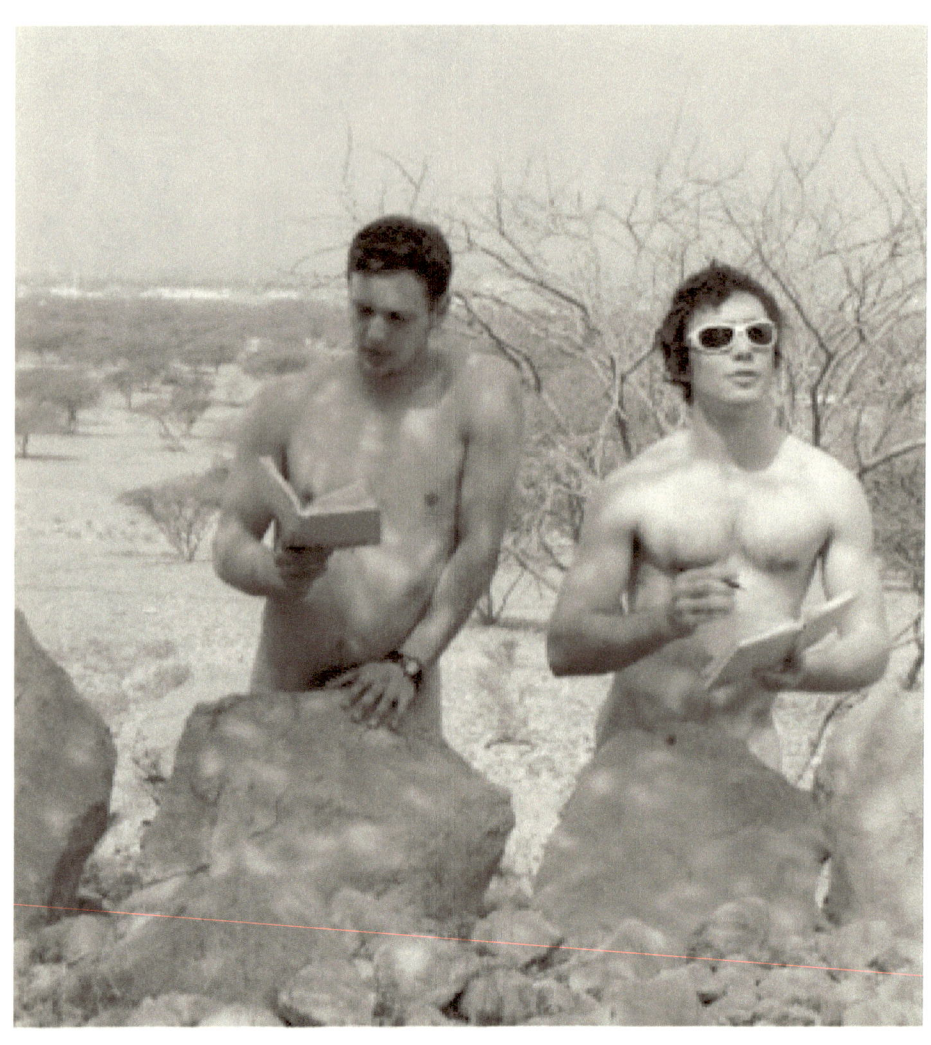

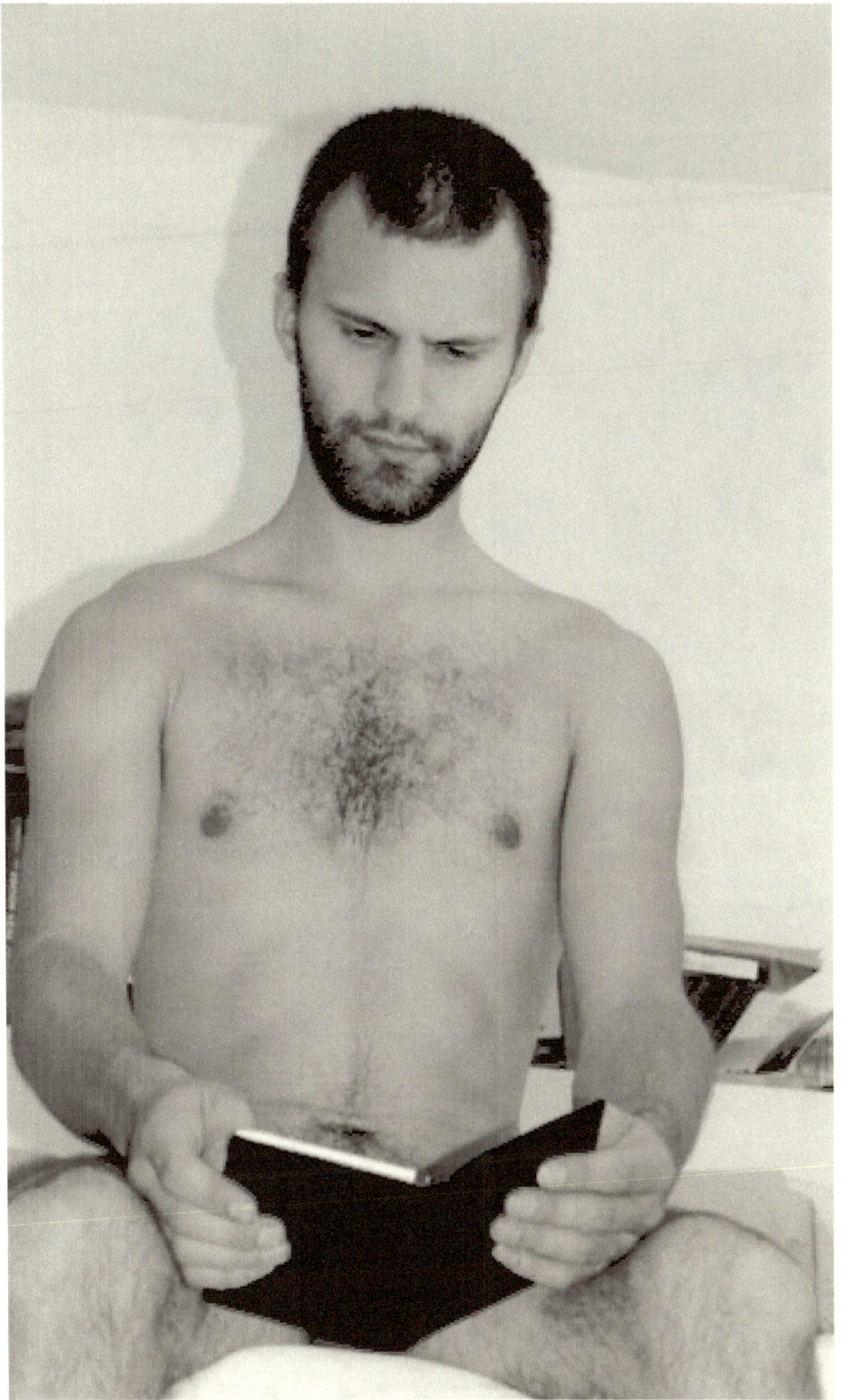

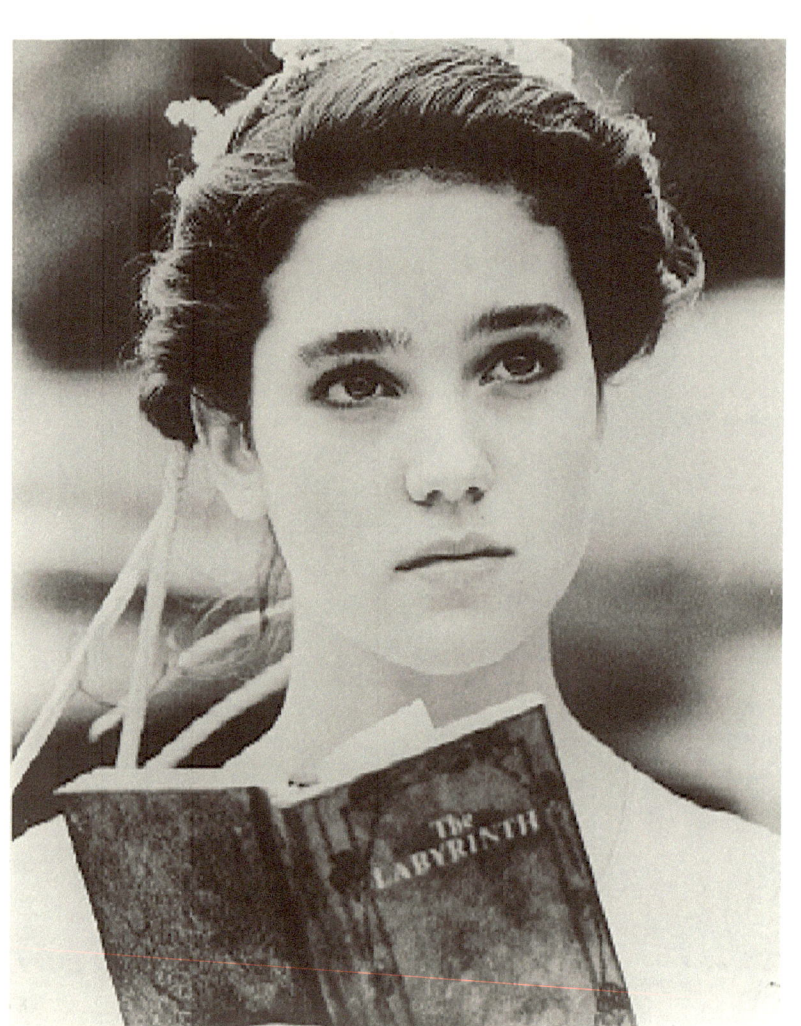

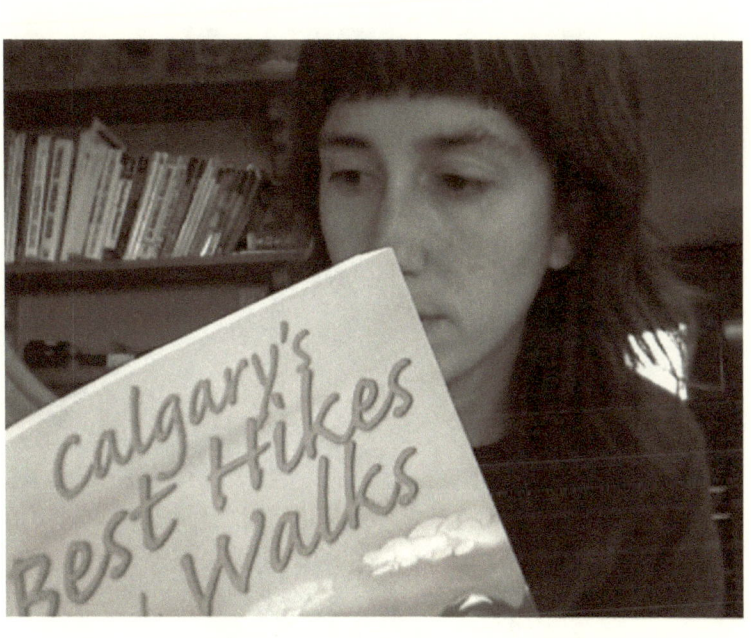

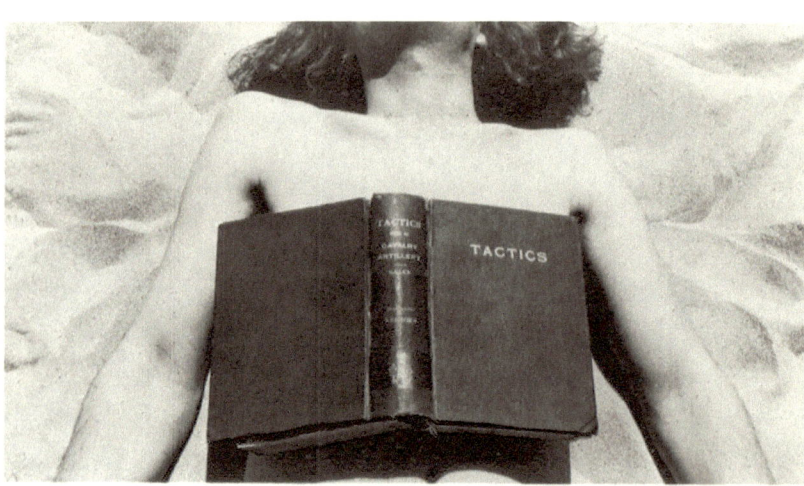
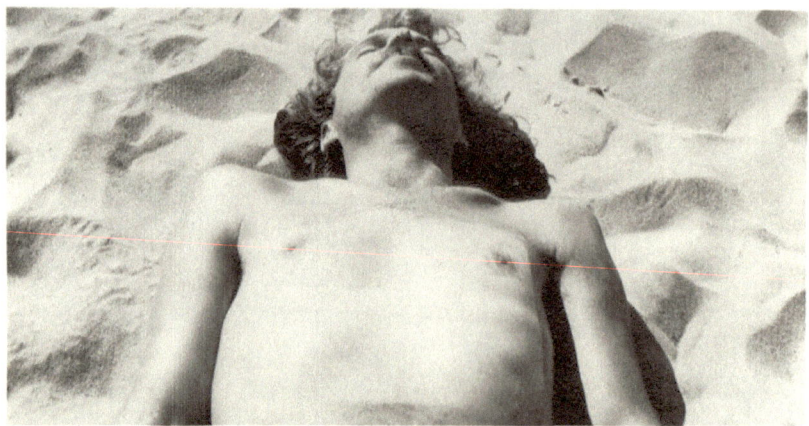

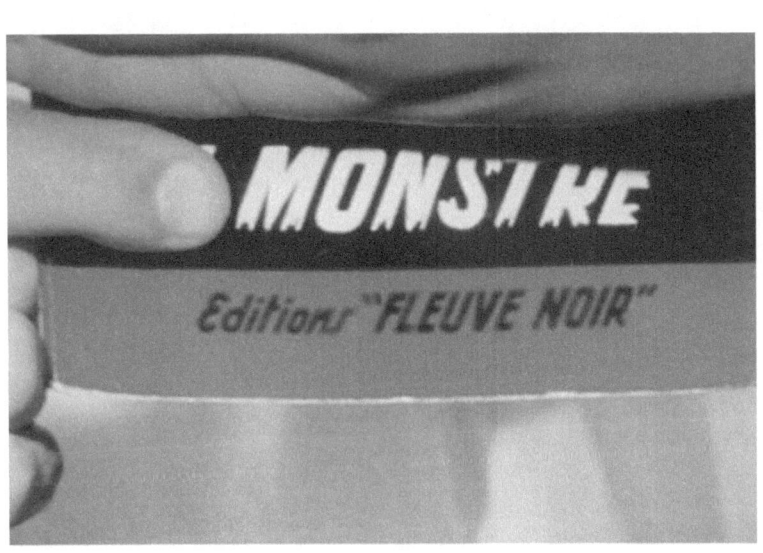

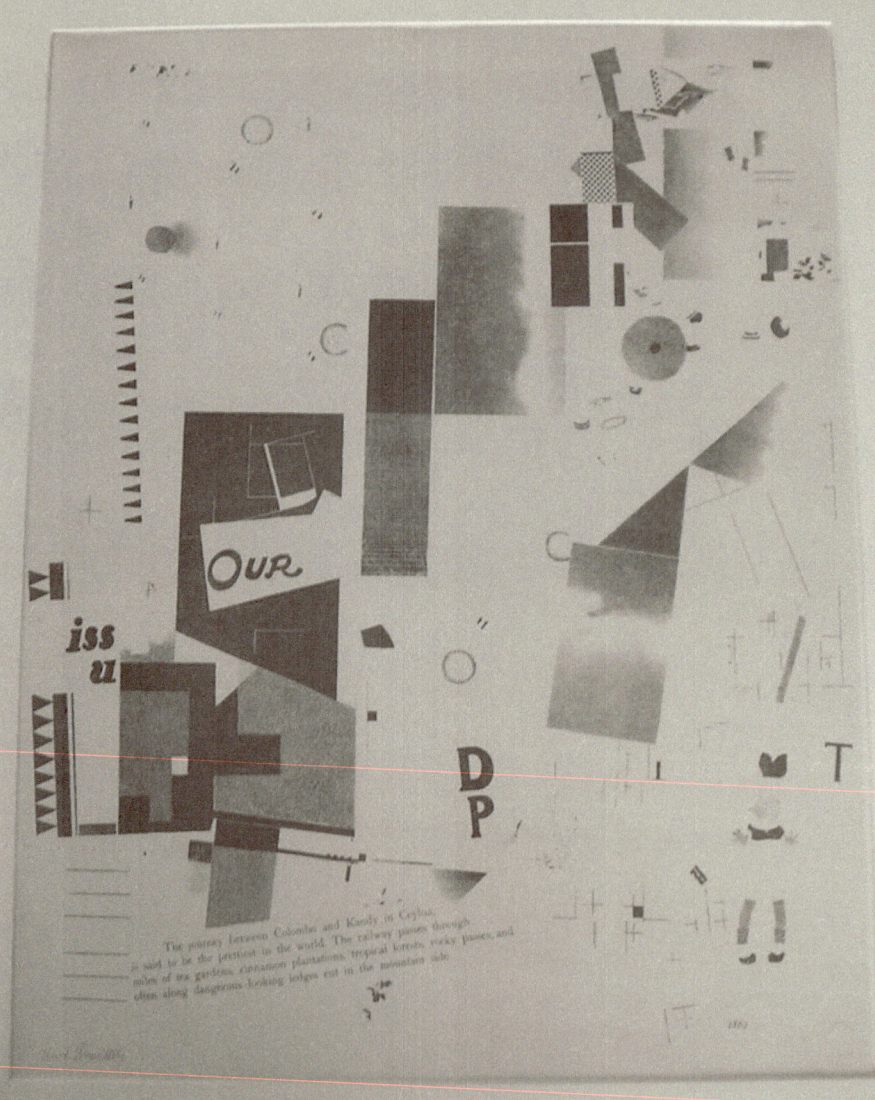

The journey between Colombo and Kandy in Ceylon, is said to be the prettiest in the world. The railway passes through miles of tea gardens, cinnamon plantations, tropical forests, rocky passes, and often along dangerous-looking ledges cut in the mountain side.

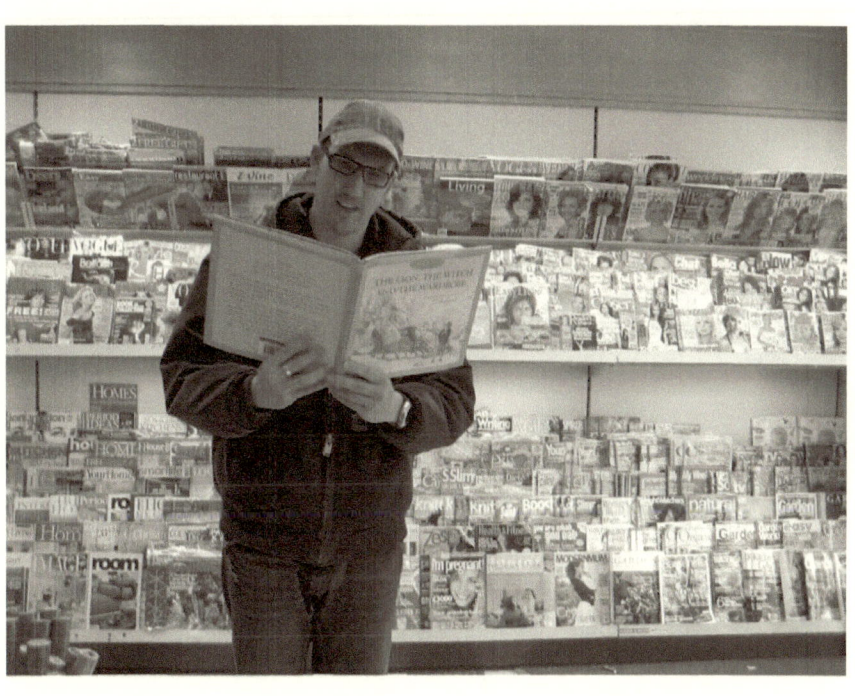

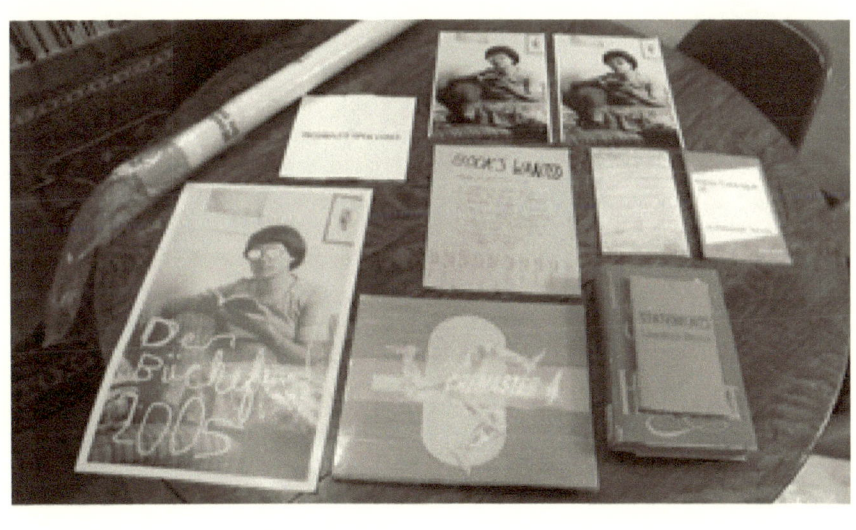

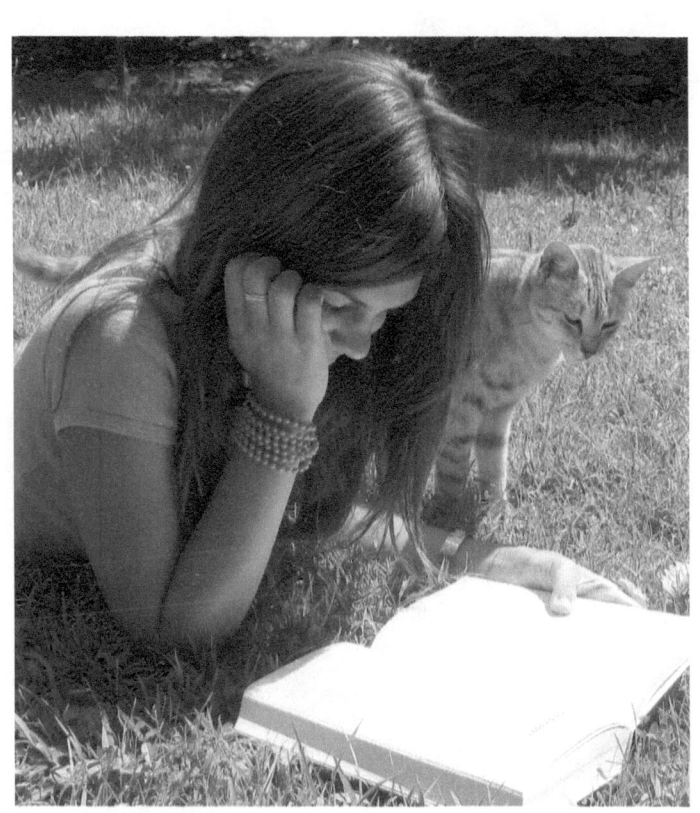

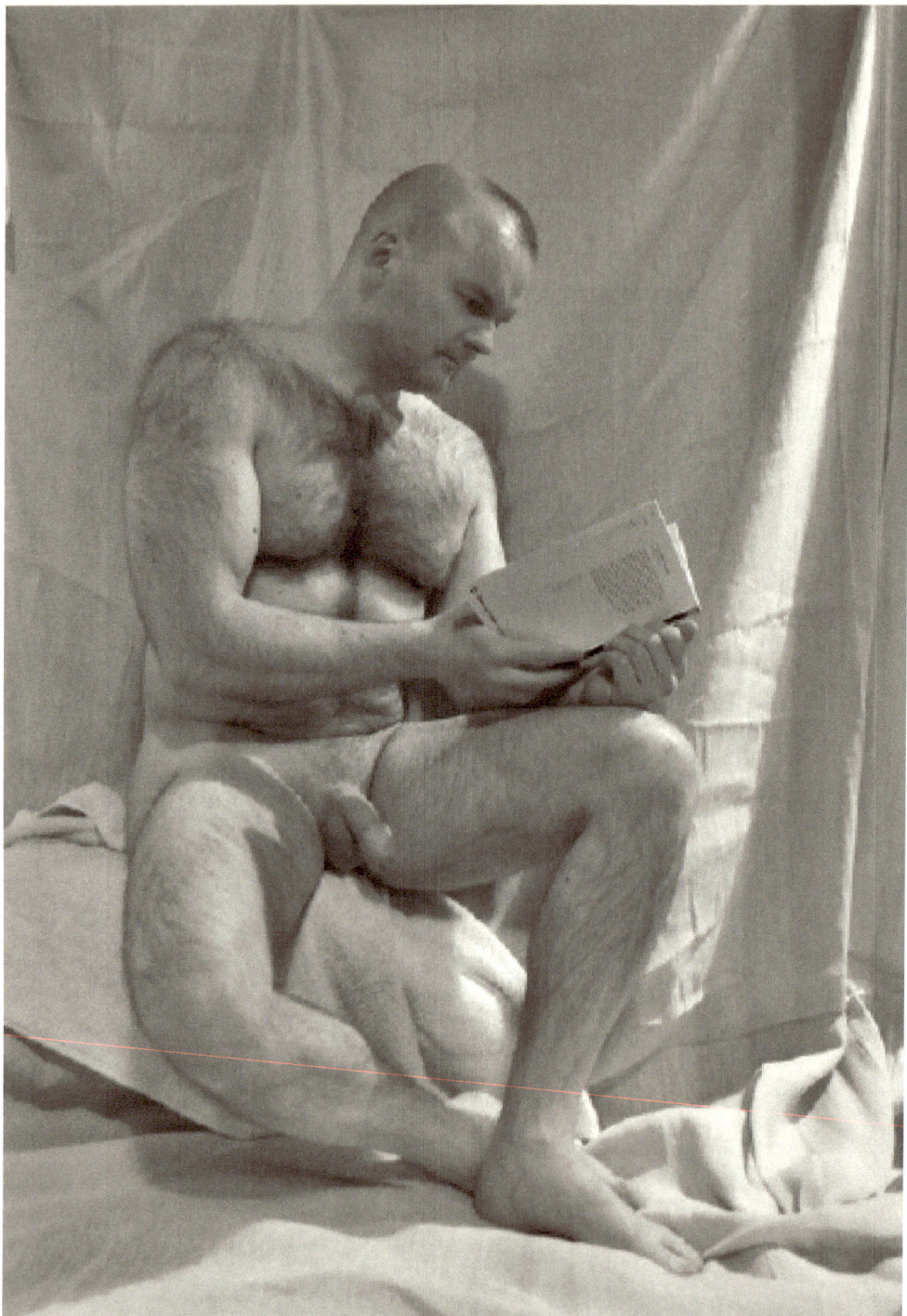

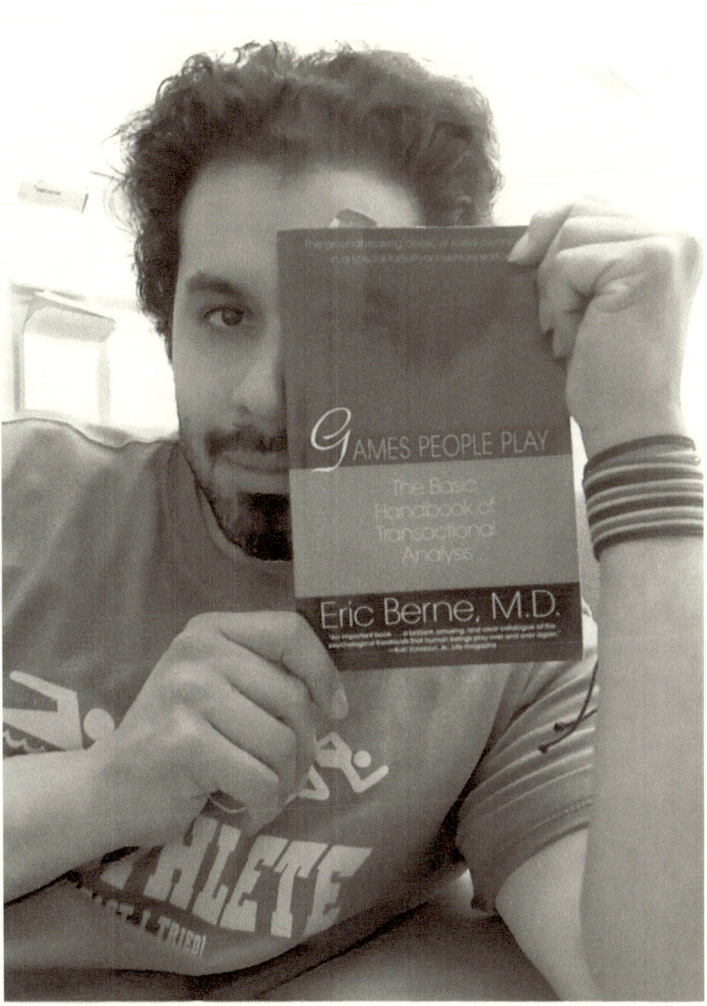

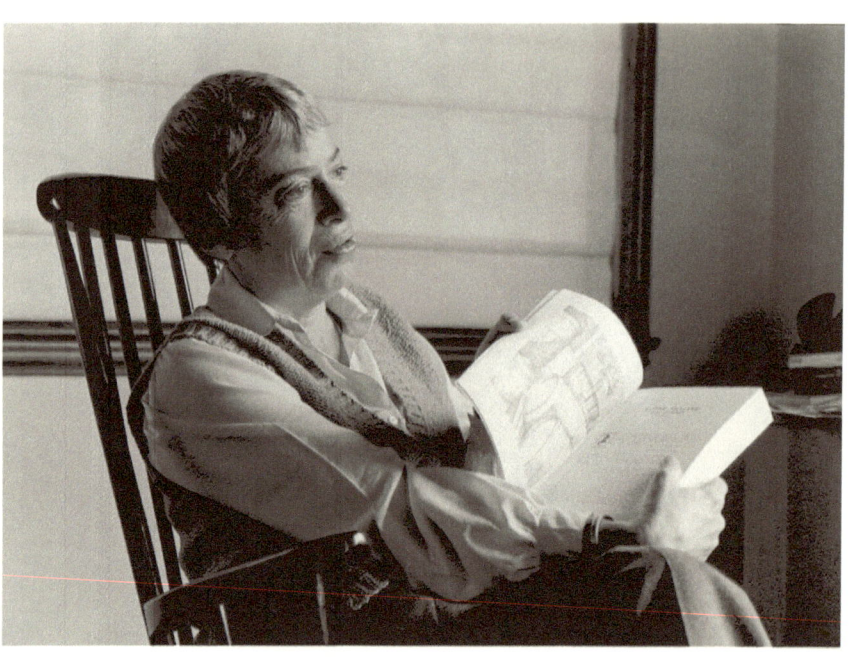

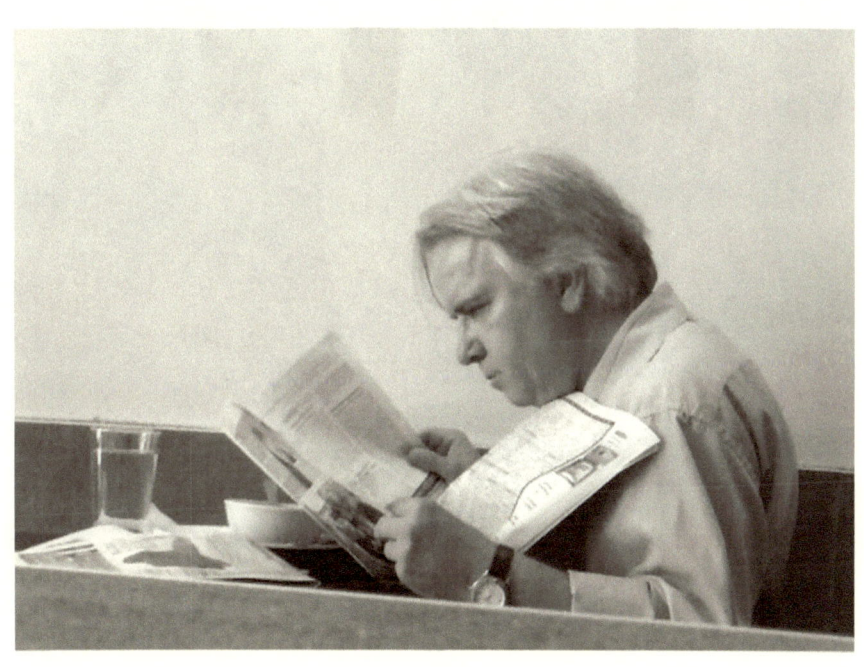

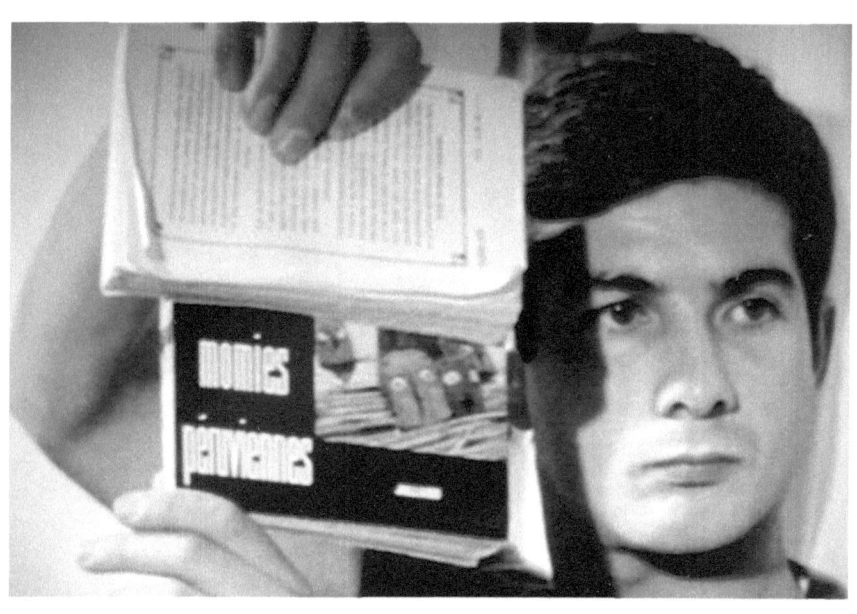

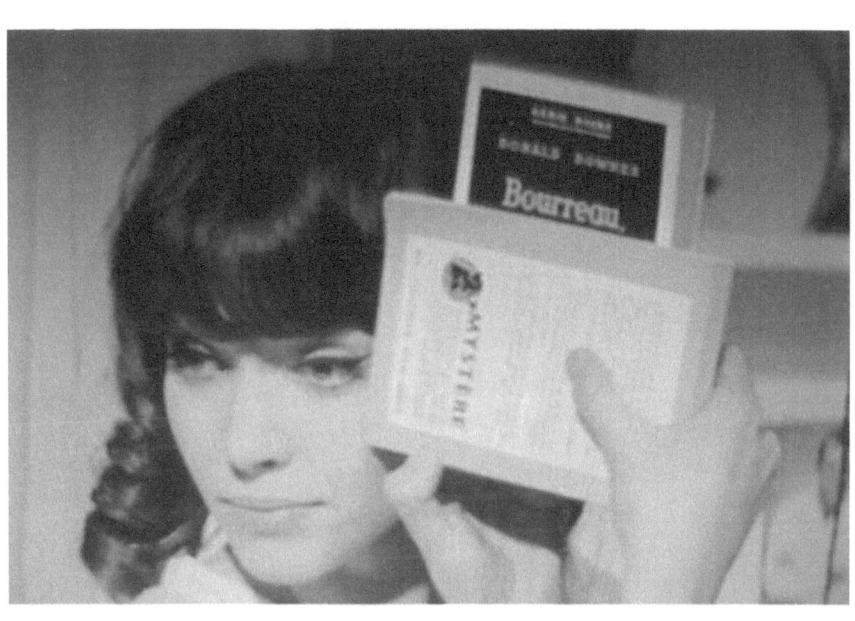

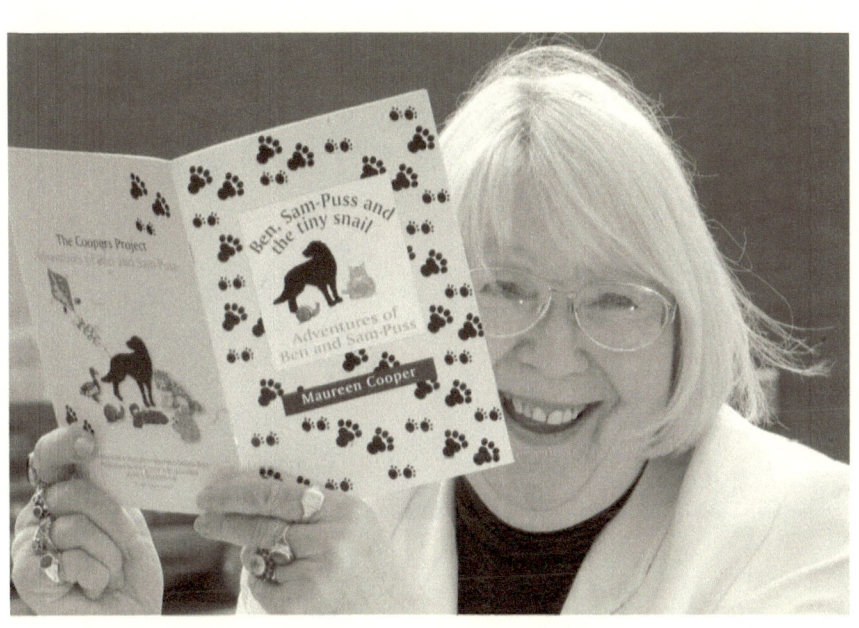

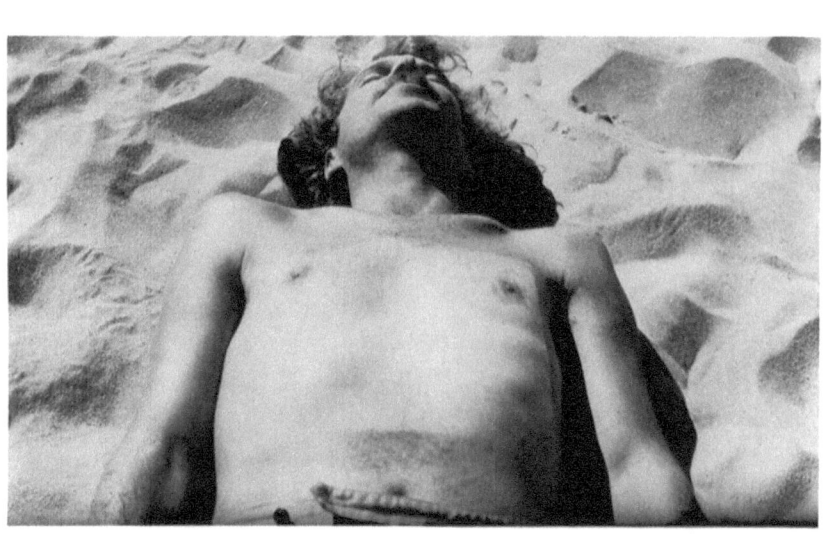

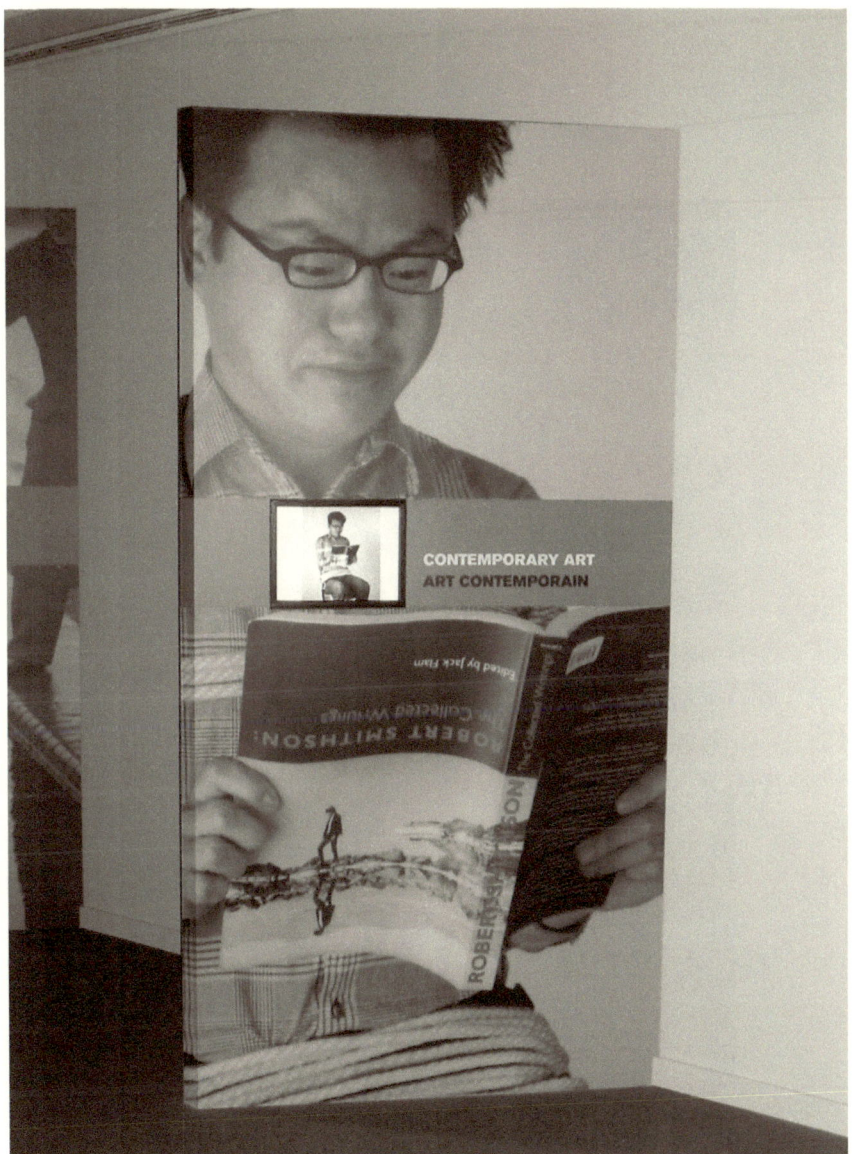

CONTEMPORARY ART
ART CONTEMPORAIN

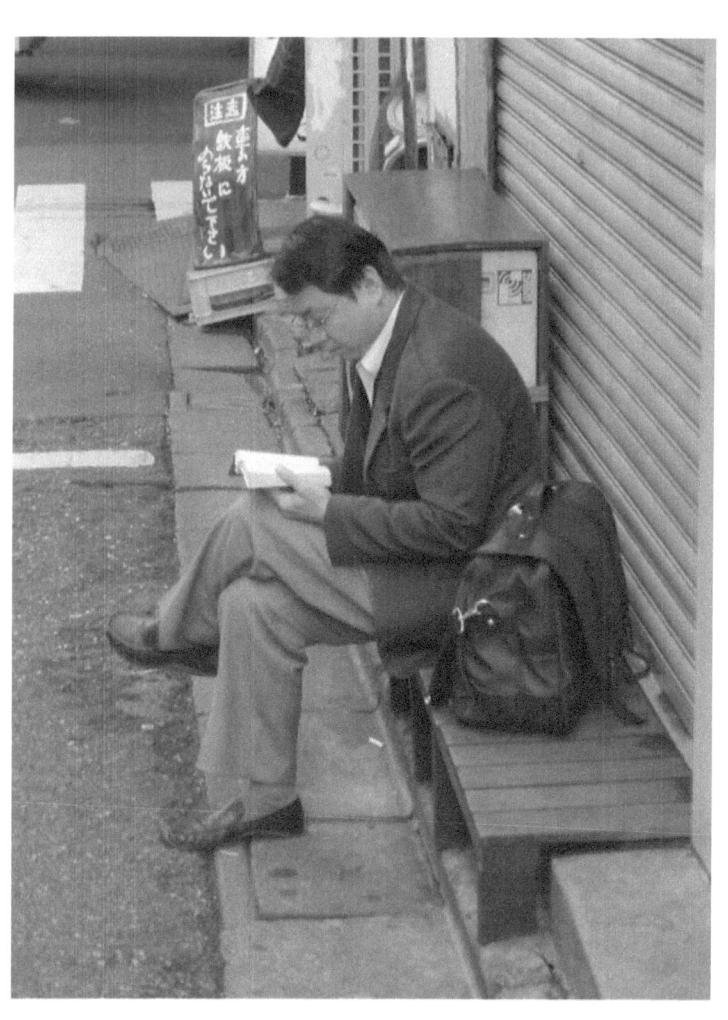

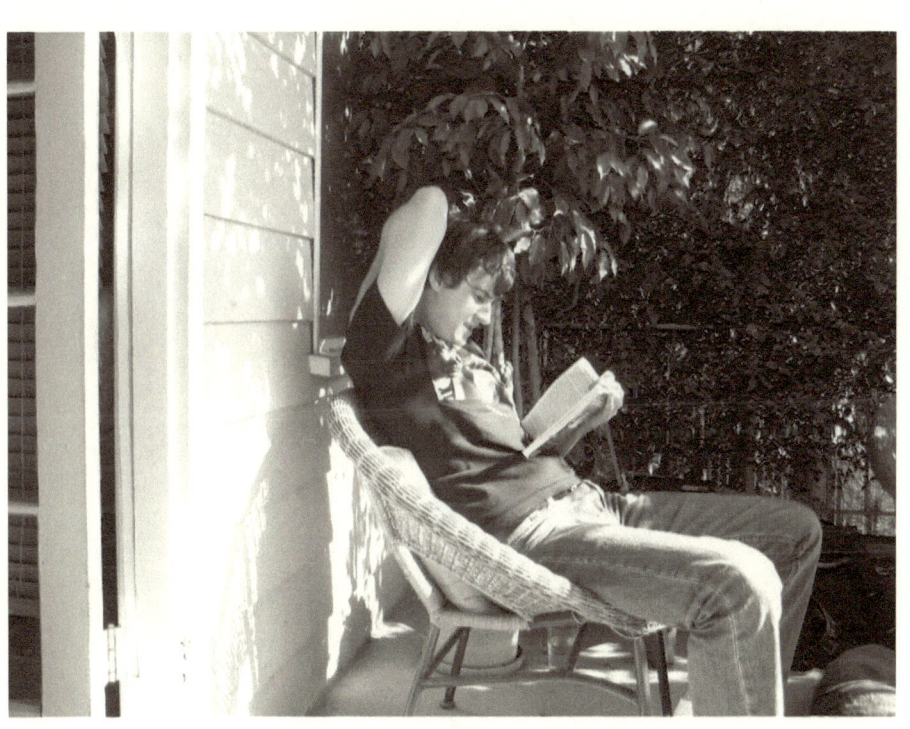

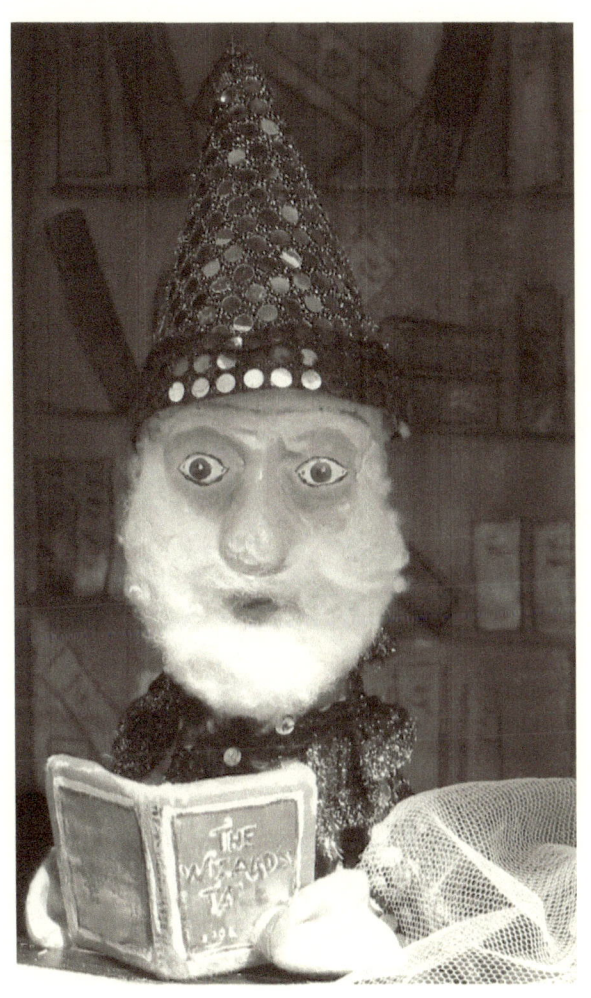

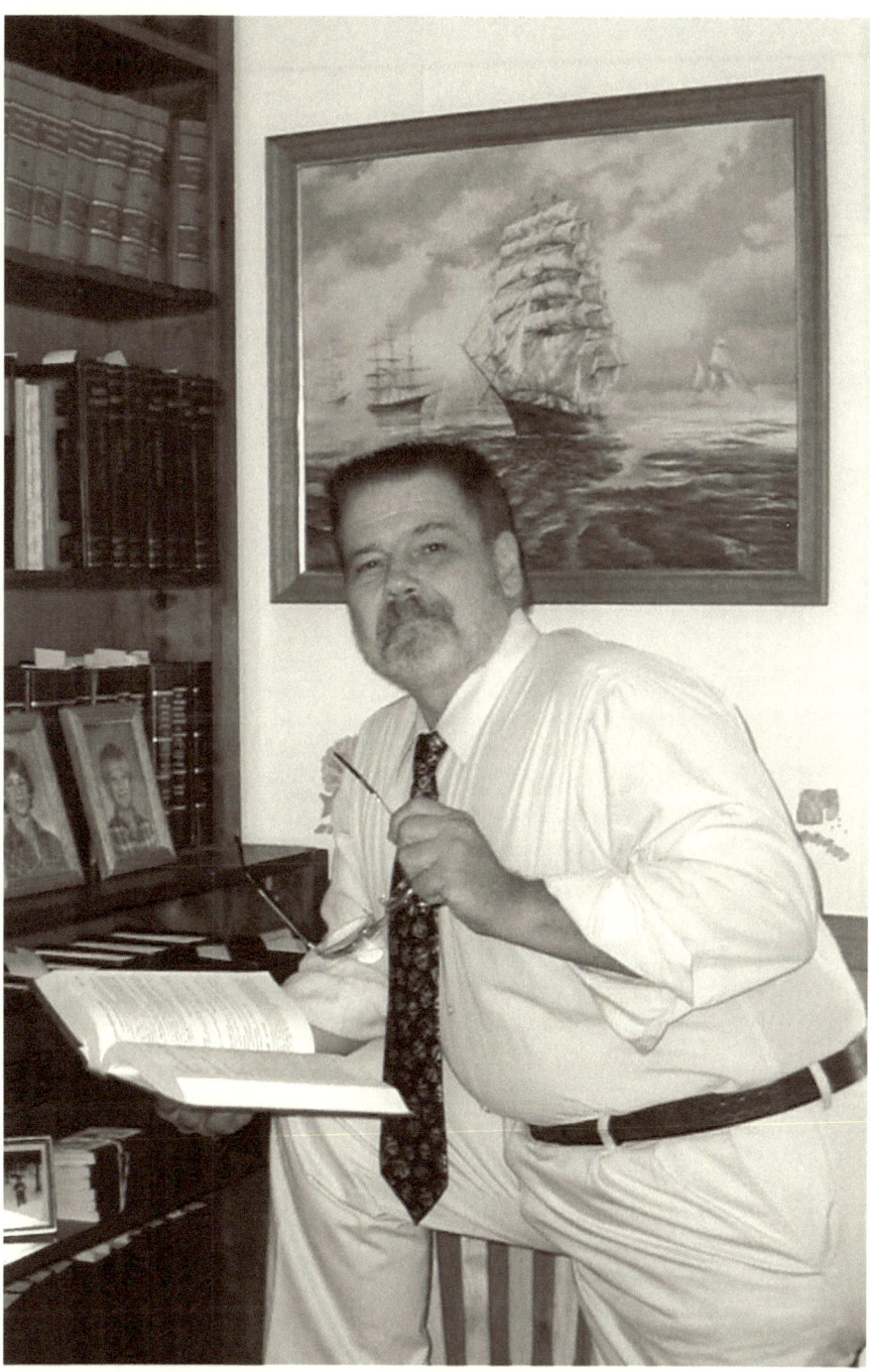

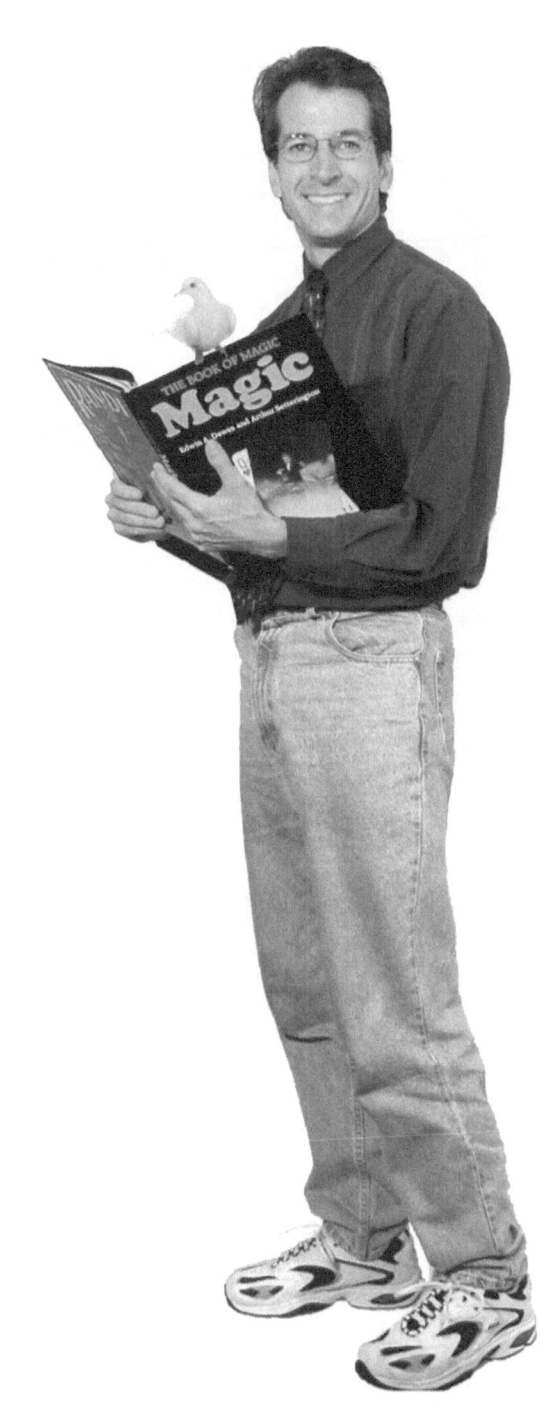

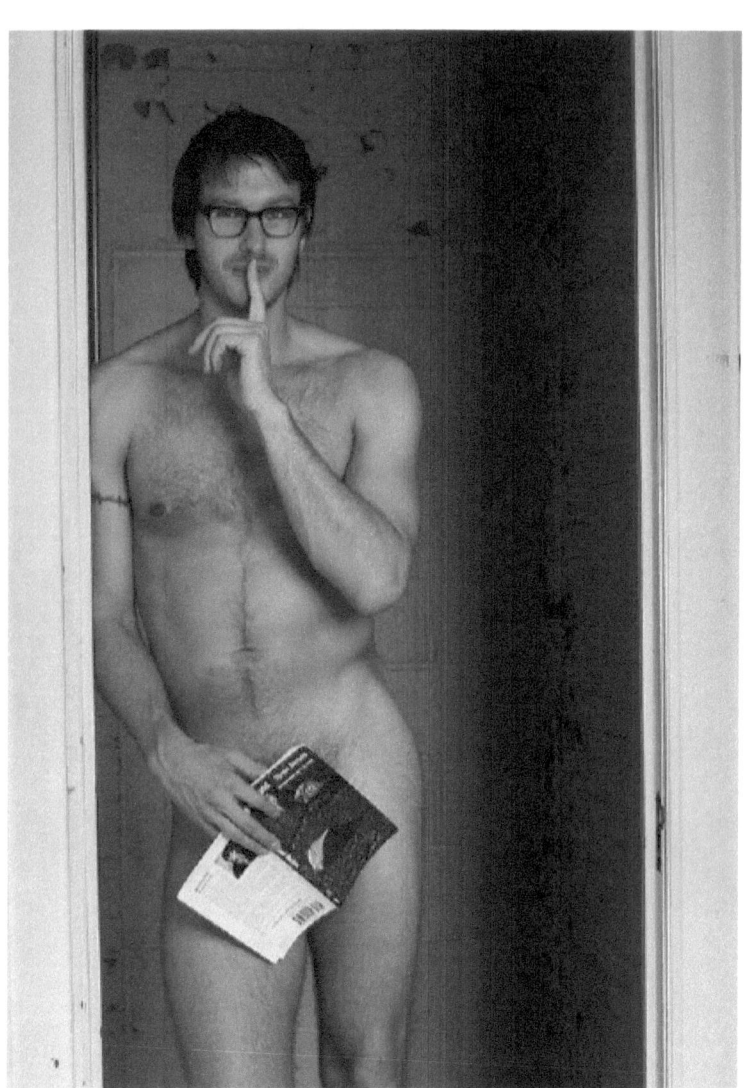

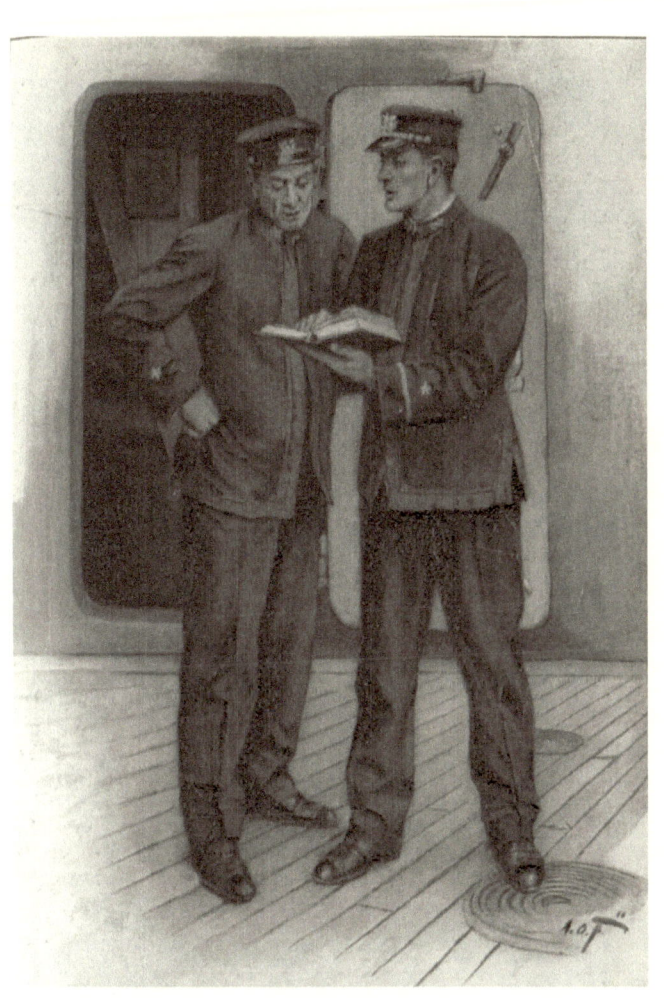

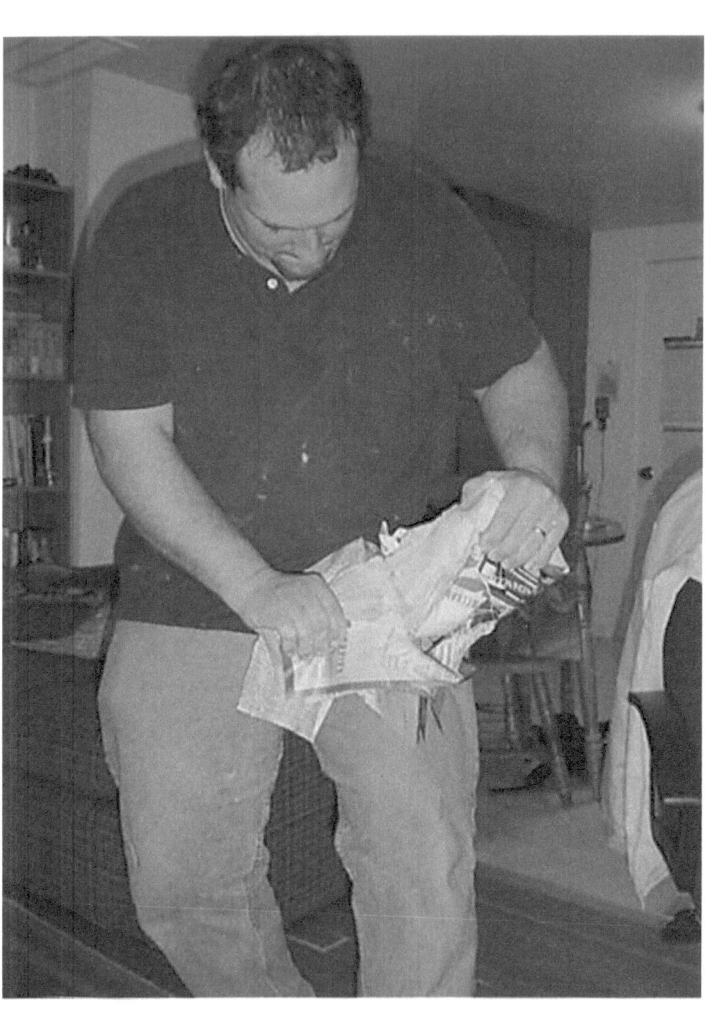

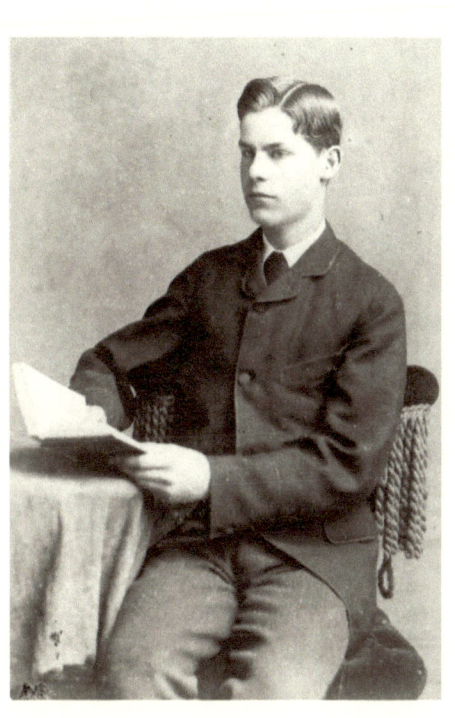

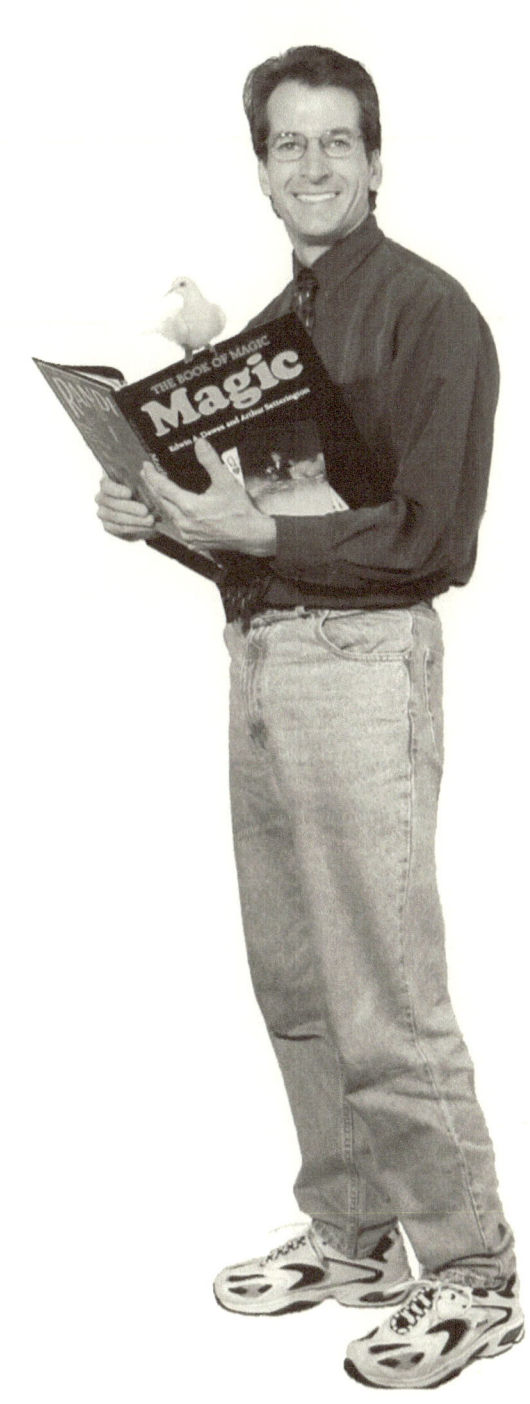

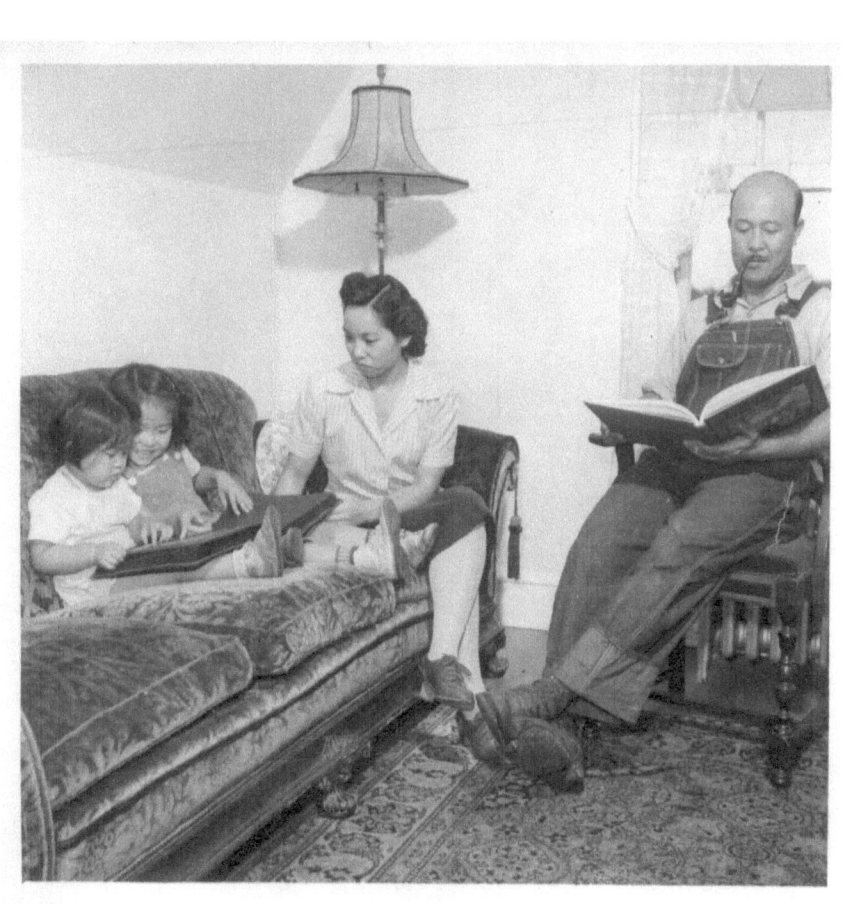

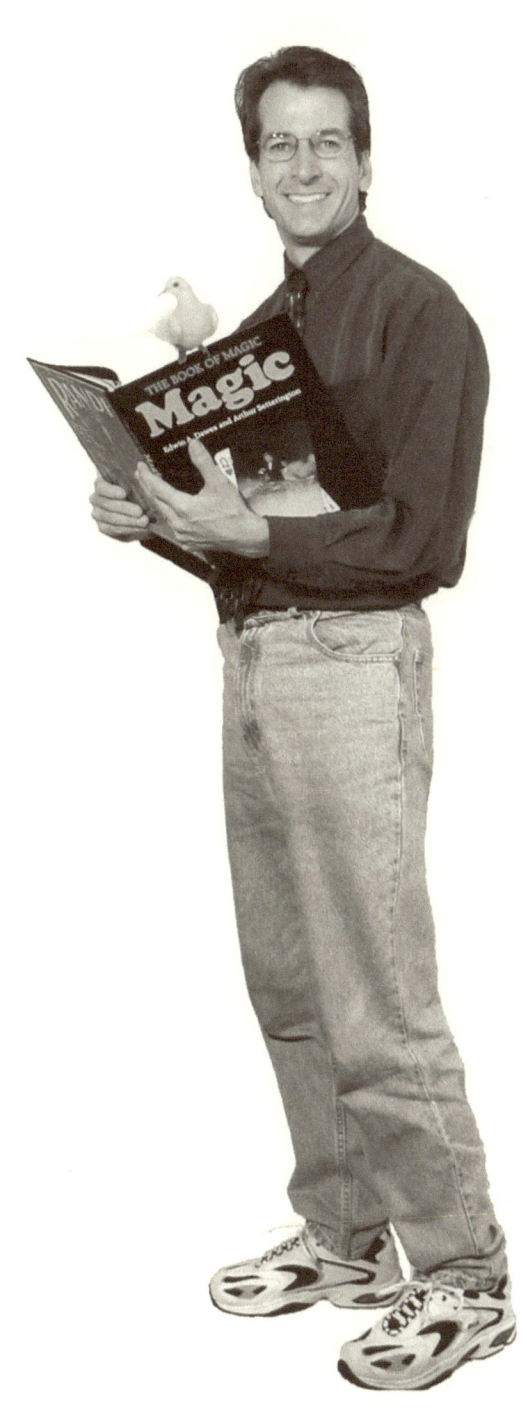

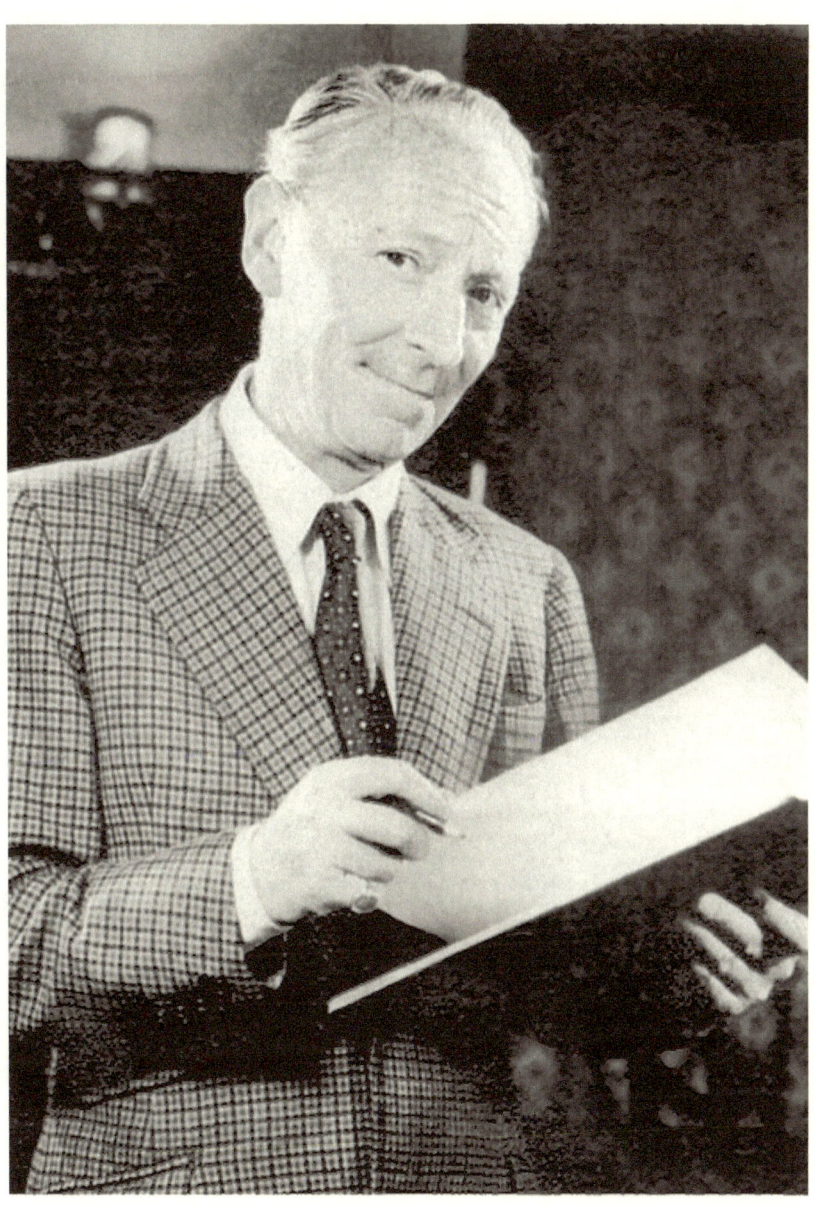

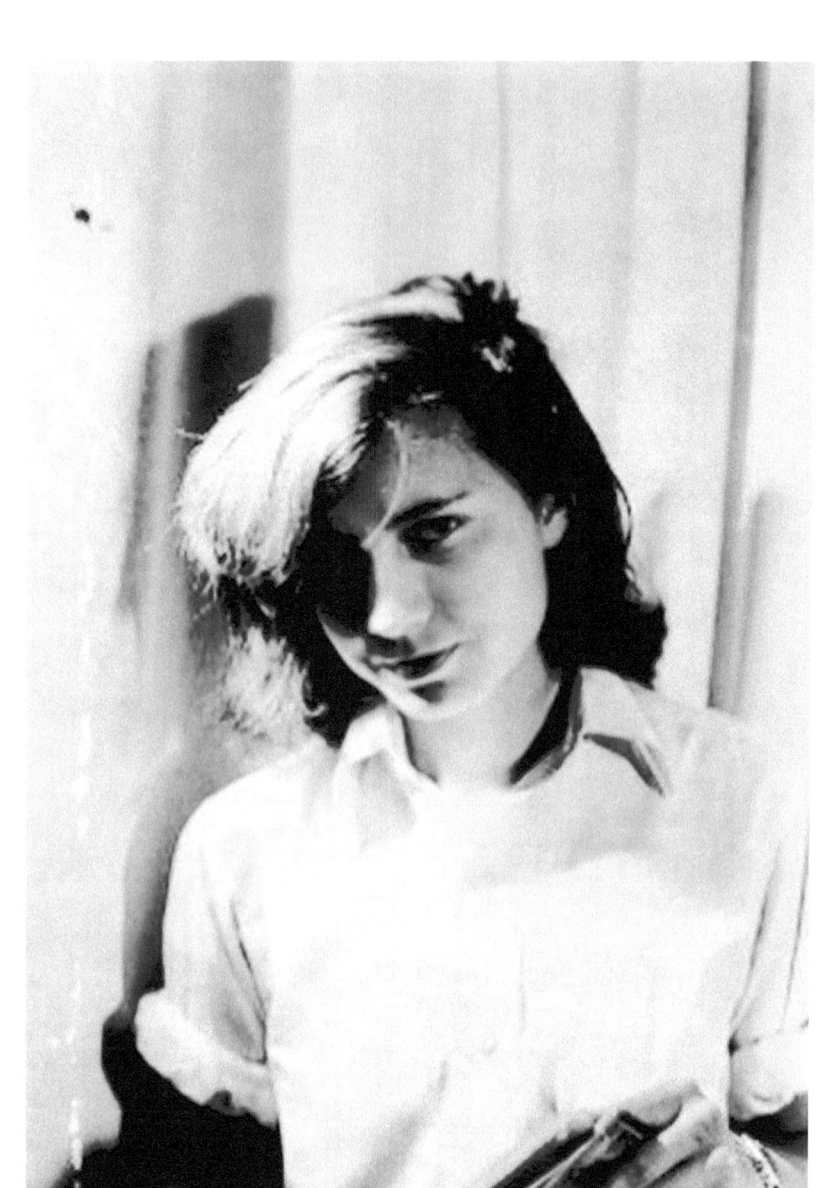

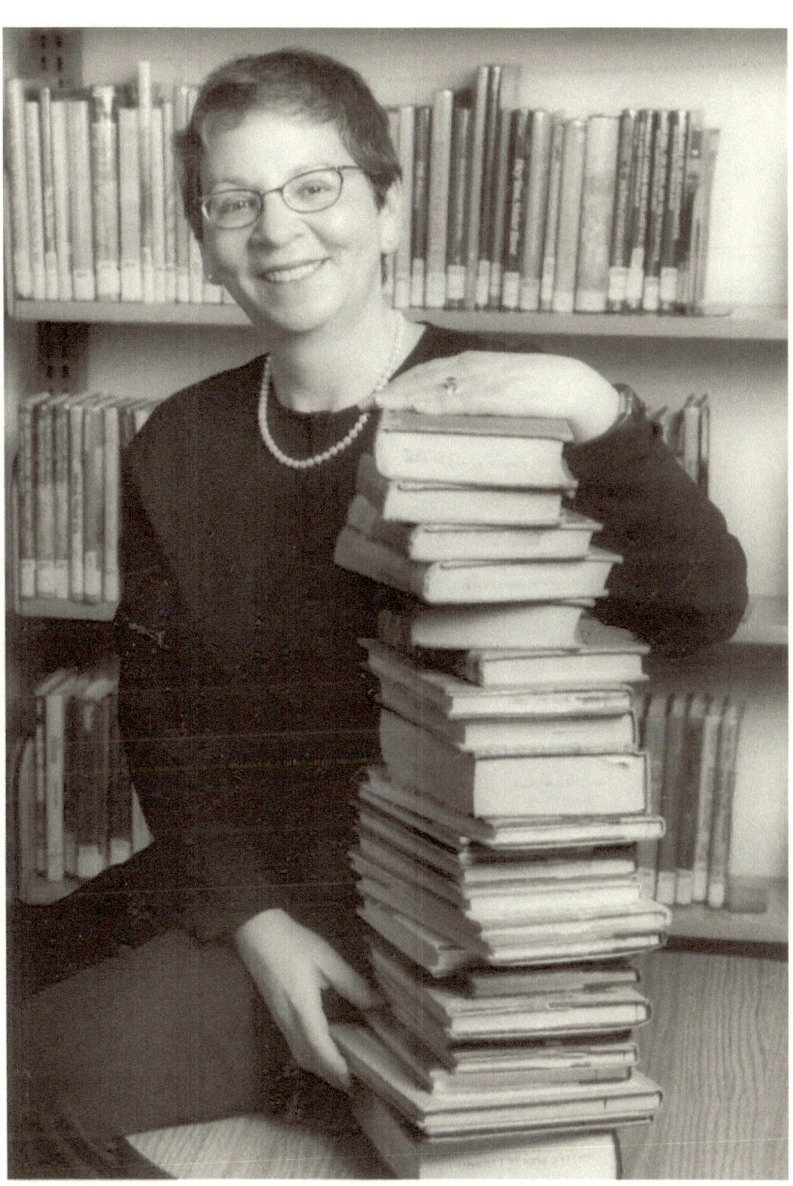

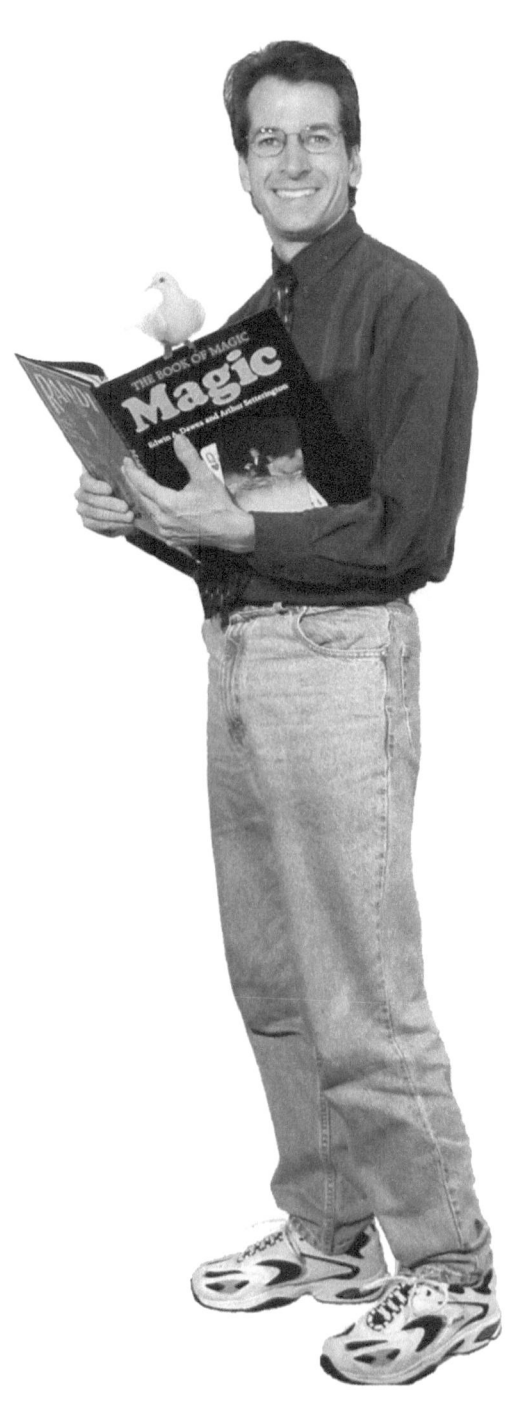

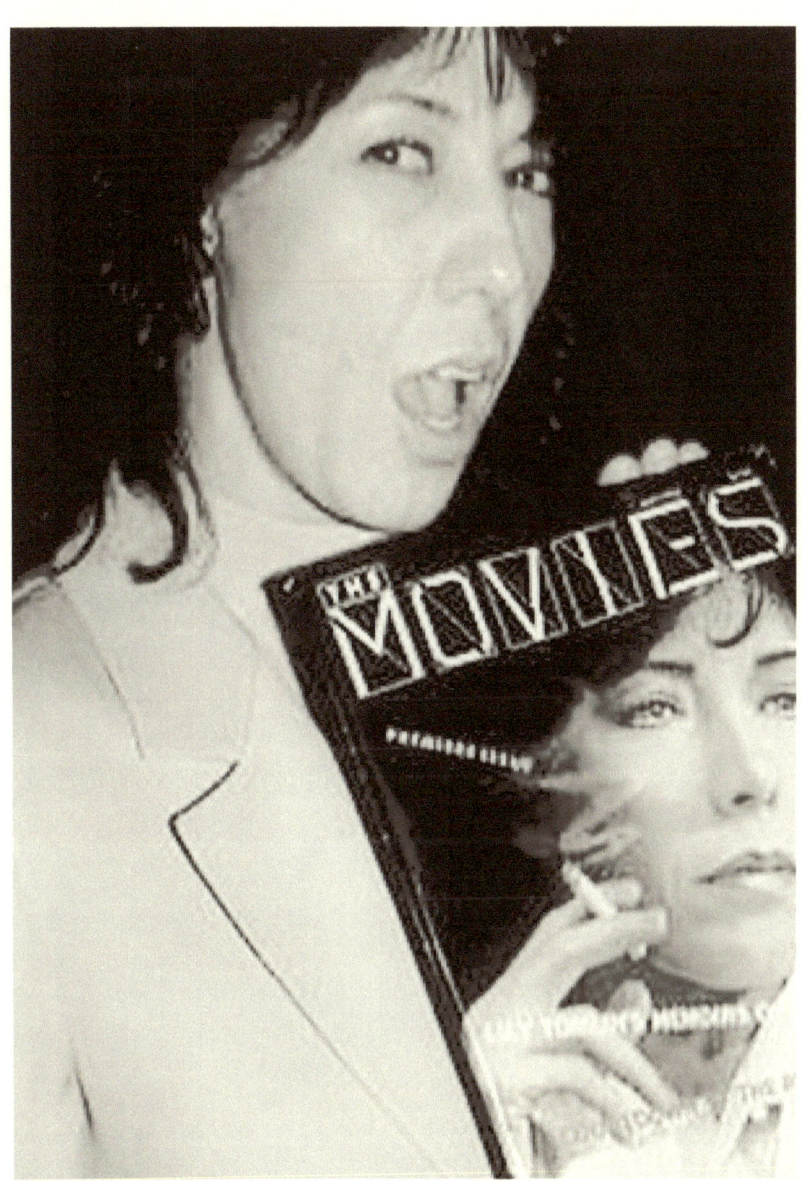

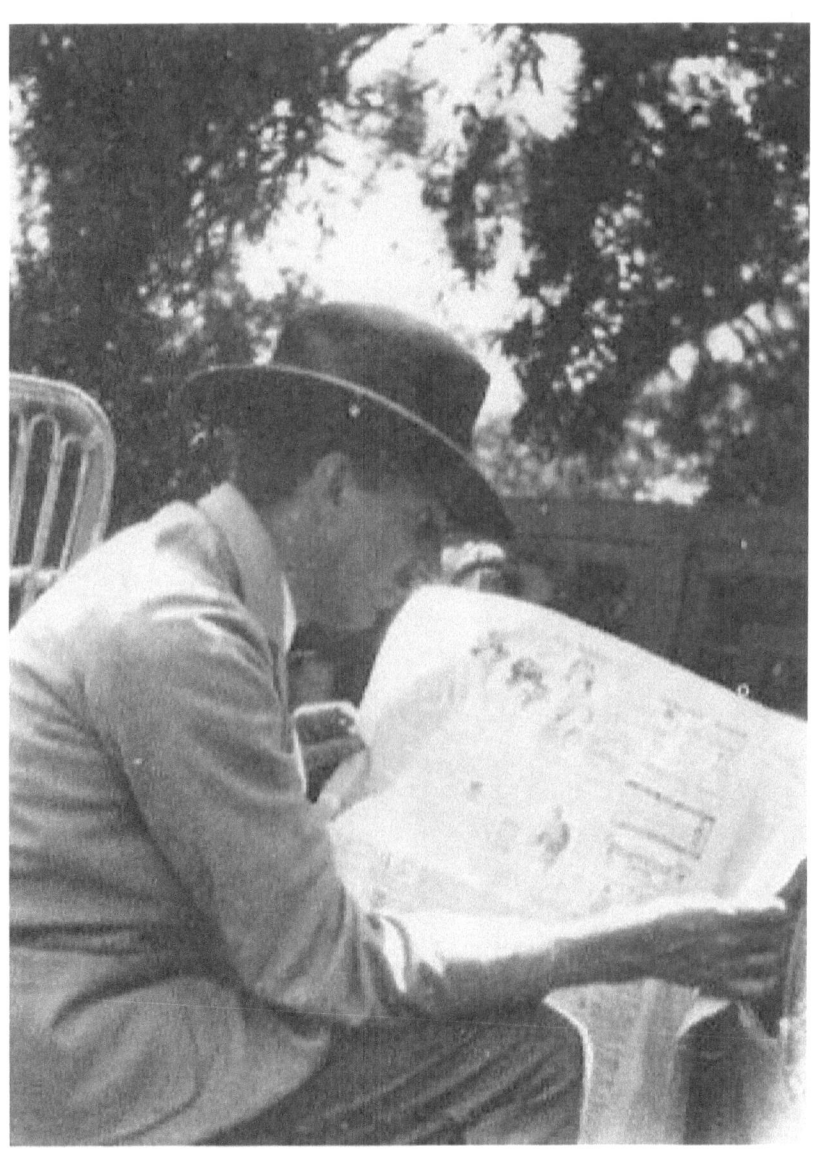

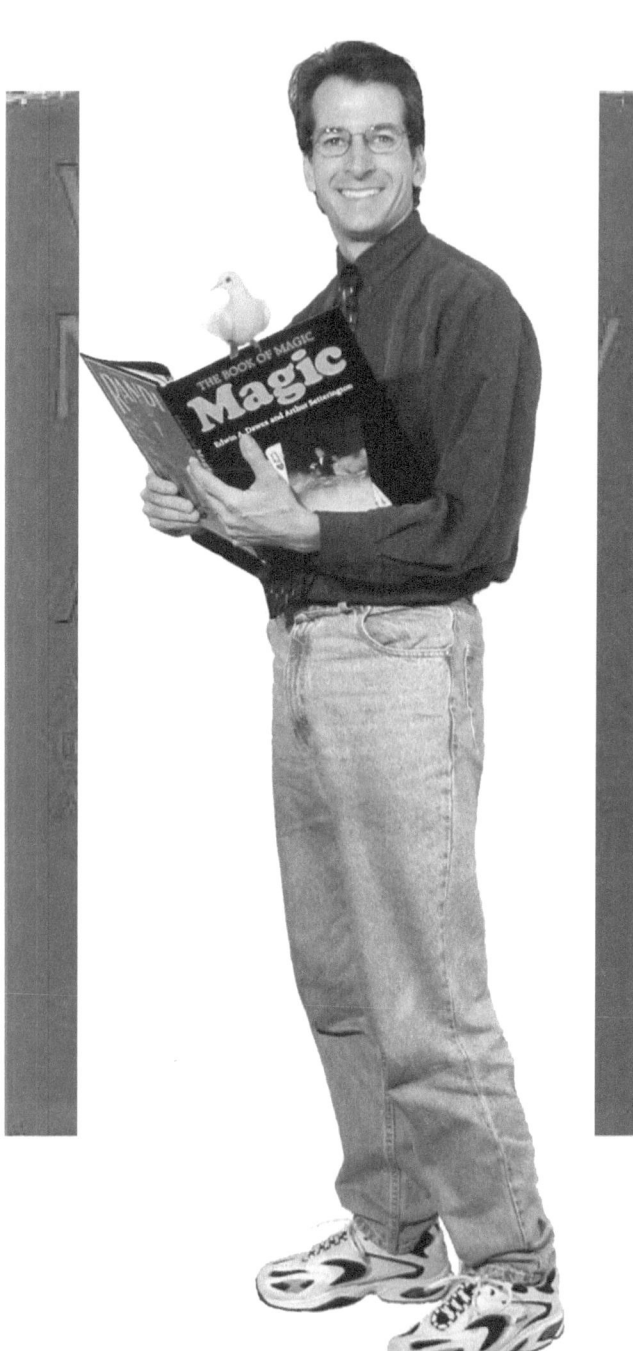

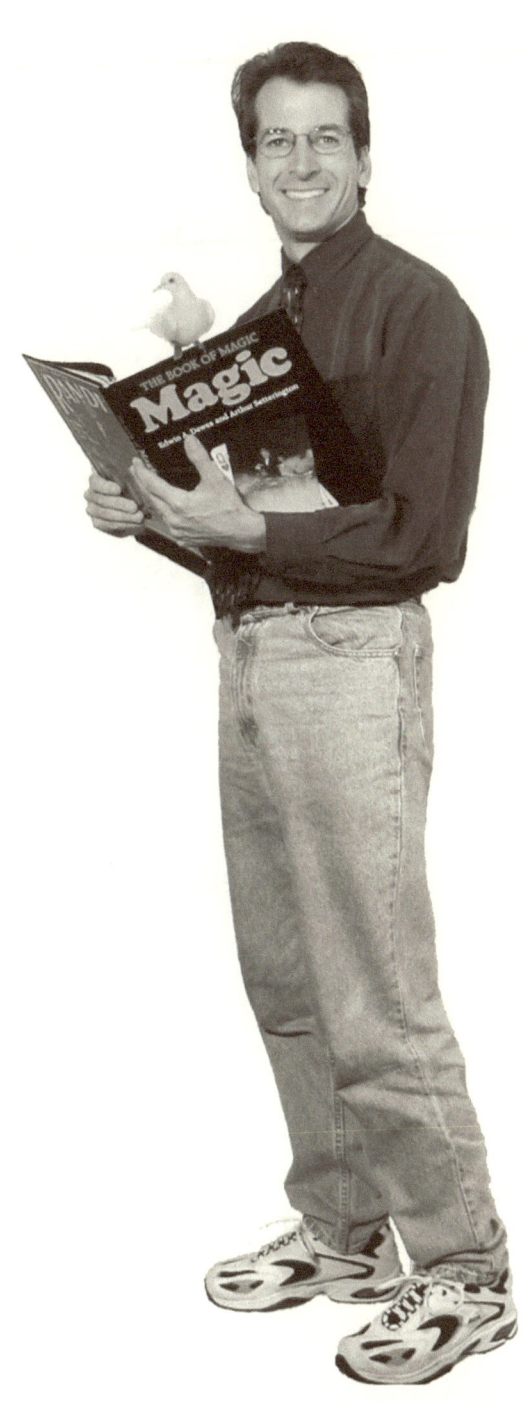

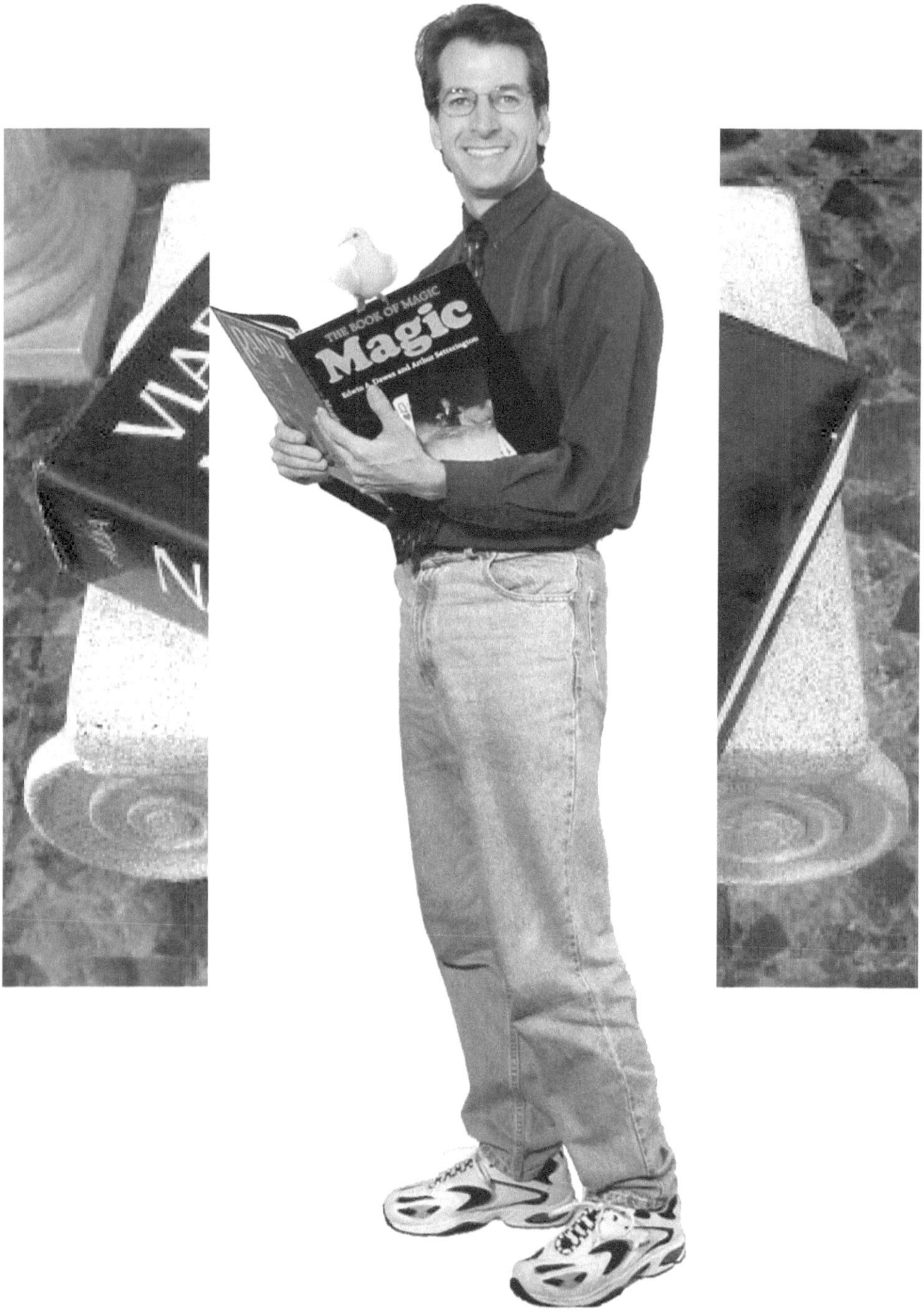

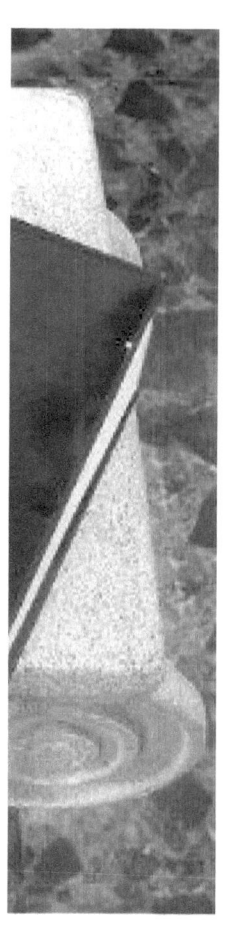

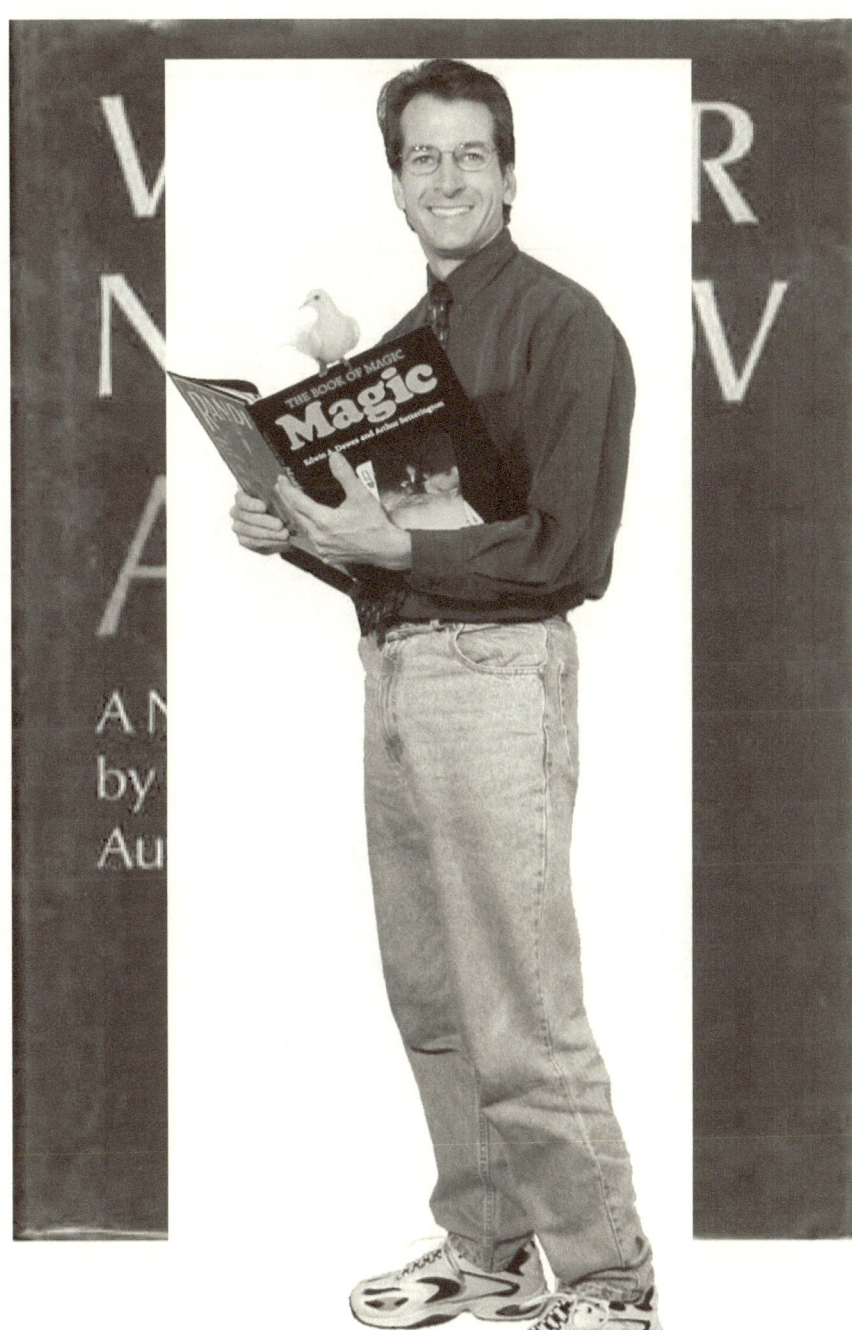

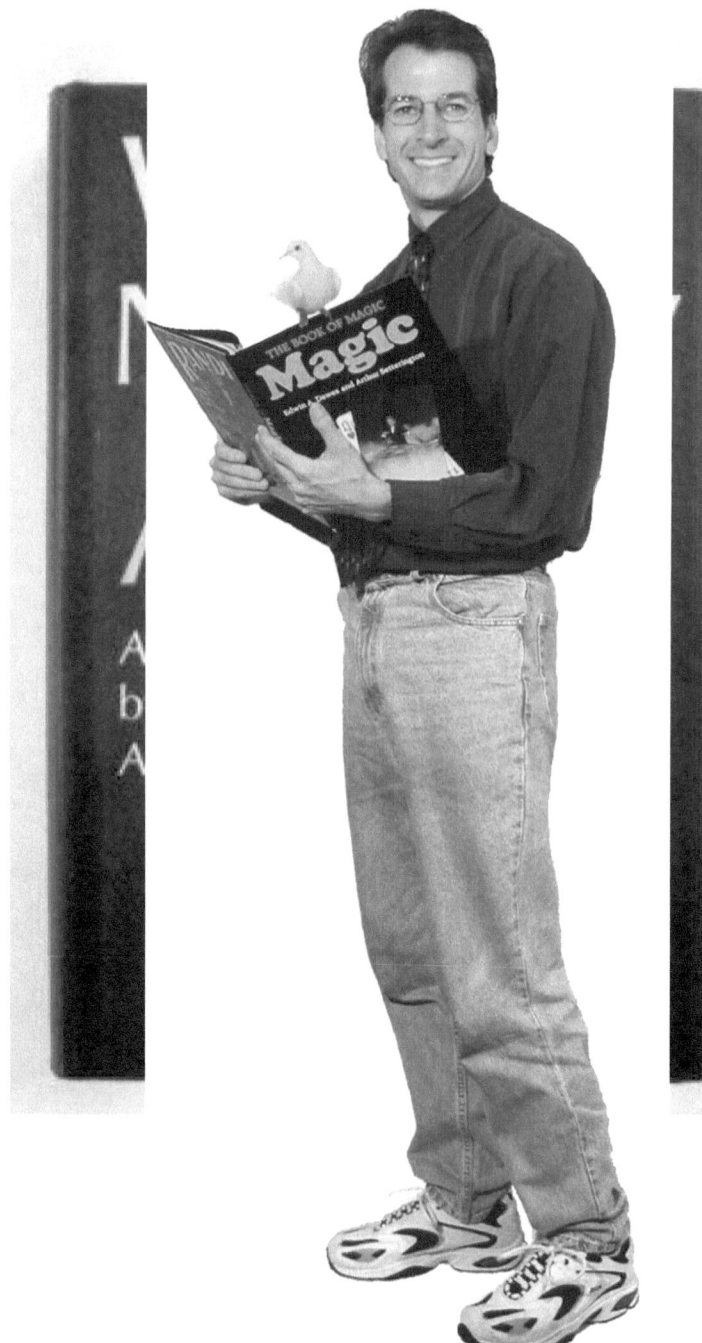

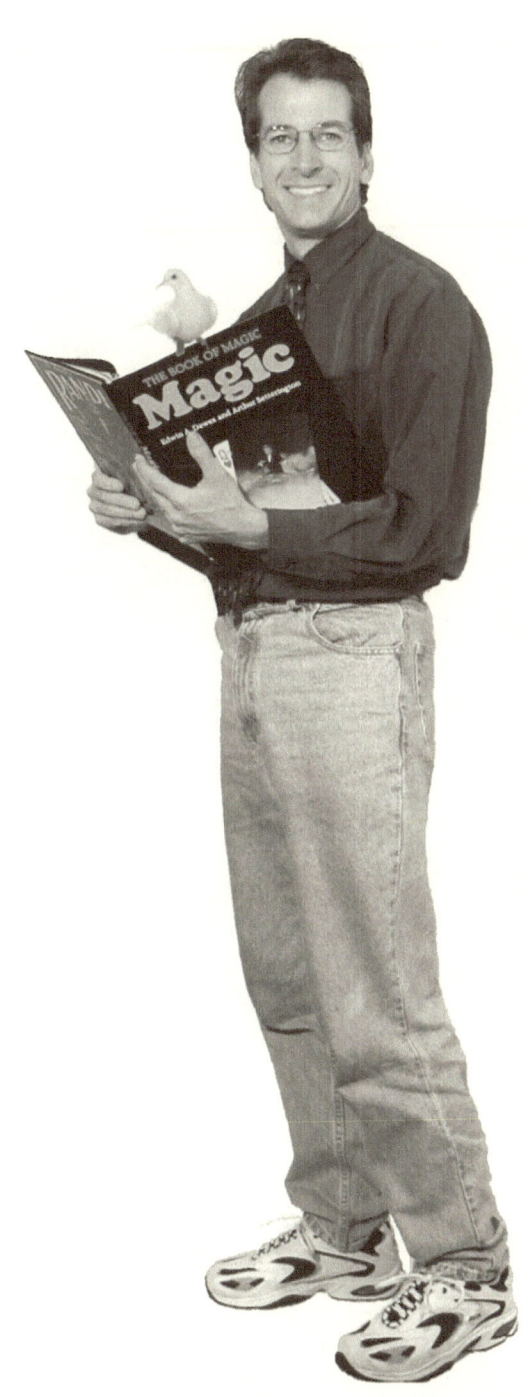

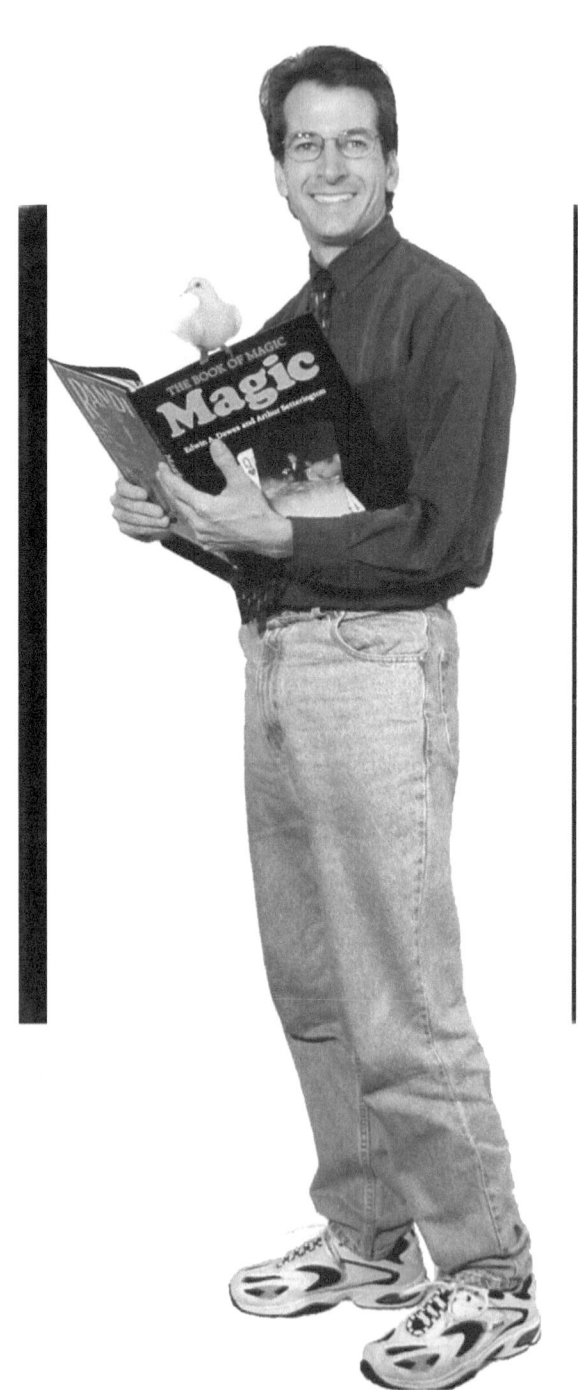

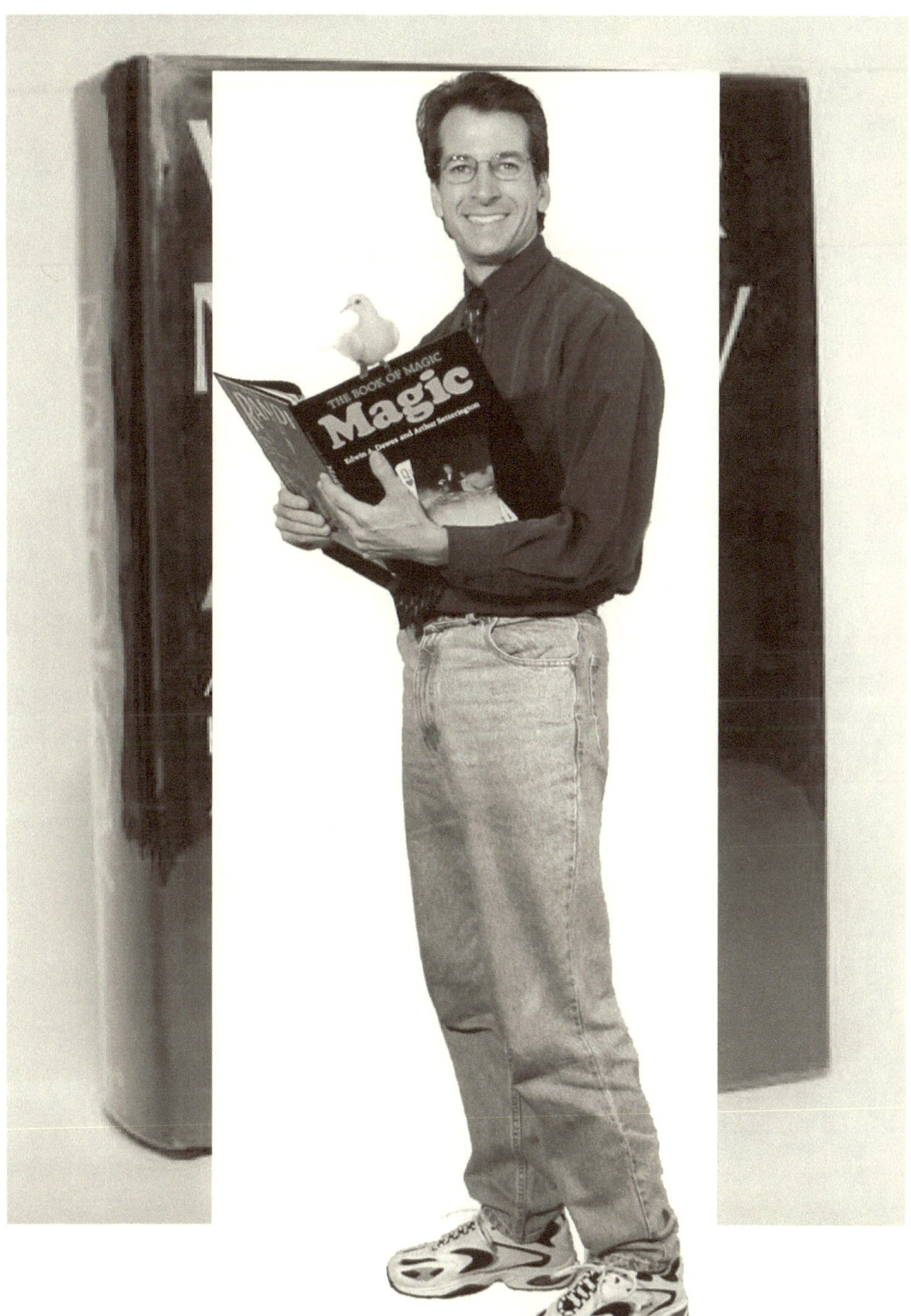

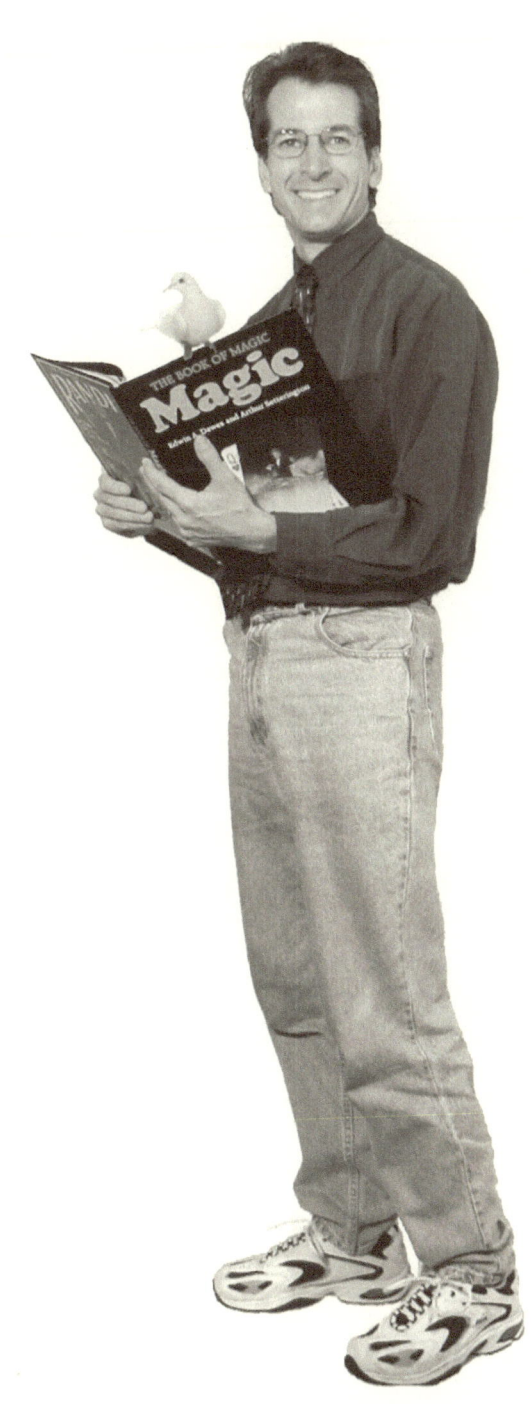

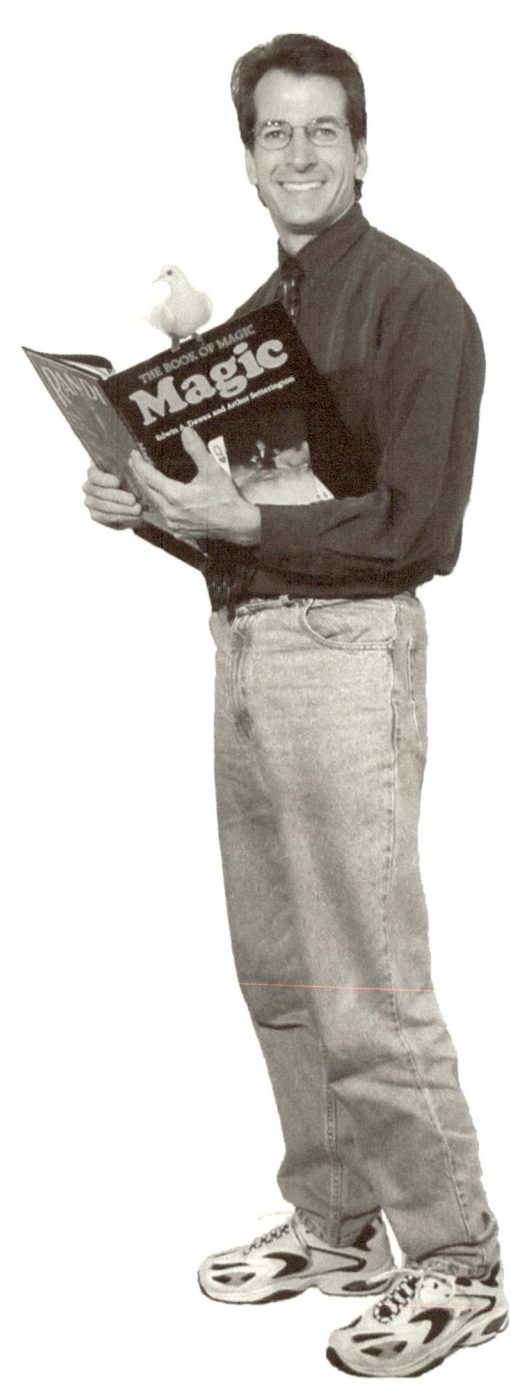

www.ingramcontent.com/pod-product-compliance
Lightning Source LLC
Chambersburg PA
CBHW021945170526
45157CB00003B/924